BAHÍYYIH KHÁNUM

Bahíyyih <u>Kh</u>ánum, from a drawing by Juliet Thompson, 1926

BAHÍYYIH KHÁNUM

The Greatest Holy Leaf

*A compilation
from Bahá'í sacred texts and writings of the Guardian
of the Faith and Bahíyyih Khánum's own letters
made by*

THE RESEARCH DEPARTMENT

at the Bahá'í World Centre

BAHÁ'Í WORLD CENTRE
HAIFA

1982

© 1982 WORLD CENTRE PUBLICATIONS

ISBN 0–85398–131–0

Printed in Great Britain

He is the Eternal! This is My testimony for her who hath heard My voice and drawn nigh unto Me. Verily, she is a leaf that hath sprung from this preexistent Root. She hath revealed herself in My name and tasted of the sweet savours of My holy, My wondrous pleasure. At one time We gave her to drink from My honeyed Mouth, at another caused her to partake of My mighty, My luminous Kawthar. Upon her rest the glory of My name and the fragrance of My shining robe.

(Bahá'u'lláh's original Arabic of the above is inscribed around the circular dome of the Greatest Holy Leaf's monument on Mount Carmel. See illustration between pages 92 and 93.)

CONTENTS

LIST OF ILLUSTRATIONS

INTRODUCTION

by

Amatu'l-Bahá Rúḥíyyih Khánum

'The outstanding heroine of the Bahá'í Dispensation.' Thus does the Guardian characterize his illustrious great-aunt, the peerless daughter of Bahá'u'lláh, the faithful and beloved sister of 'Abdu'l-Bahá. In this compilation presented by the Universal House of Justice on the occasion of the 50th anniversary of the death of the Greatest Holy Leaf, Bahíyyih Khánum, the Tablets written by Bahá'u'lláh and 'Abdu'l-Bahá and the letters written by Shoghi Effendi, the Guardian, have been assembled and many of the letters which she herself wrote have been included. Because of their nature they are not a history but rather an insight into a glorious period of history.

The Greatest Holy Leaf was the eldest daughter of Bahá'u'lláh, the Founder of the Bahá'í Faith. Born in Persia in 1846 she, in her long life which ended in 1932, spanned, with the exception of two years, the entire Heroic Age of this new world religion. At the age of six when her Father was cast into the subterranean dungeon in Ṭihrán known as the 'Black Hole', her home was immediately looted and despoiled. In a day the wealthy and noble family was beggared and hid in fear of their lives as Bahá'u'lláh lay in heavy chains—the most prominent, the most blameless victim of the turmoil which His Forerunner's liberal teachings had provoked in a land of bitter Muslim Shí'ah fanaticism. Navváb, the refined, frail, saintly mother of the little girl fled to a humble dwelling near the dungeon where she could be near her illustrious and much-loved Spouse; 'Abdu'l-Bahá, her eight-year-old Brother, accompanied His mother when daily she went to the home of friends to ascertain whether Bahá'u'lláh was still alive or had been executed that day— for every day some of His co-religionists were martyred, often being handed over to various guilds, the butchers, the bakers, the shoemakers, the blacksmiths, who exercised their ingenuity on new ways of torturing them to death. Through long days of constant terror the little girl stayed at home with her four-year-old brother Mihdí; often, she recalled, she could hear the shrieks of the mob as they carried off their victims. After four months Bahá'u'lláh was released through the intervention of various prominent people, and He and His family were exiled to 'Iráq. In a very severe winter, through the snow-bound mountains of western Persia, the ill-clad, destitute party for three months suffered the ordeal of what He described as *'that terrible journey'*. Navváb sold the gold buttons of her clothes to help buy food and washed their garments till her delicate hands bled. Such were the earliest recollections of Bahíyyih Khánum; the happy, secure days of her first six years must have become a dream-like experience, for no real peace ever entered her life again. Her Brother 'Abdu'l-Bahá testified to this: *'For all her days she was denied a moment of tranquillity.'*

The family had barely settled in Baghdád when the infant Faith of Bahá'u'lláh was seized by a new convulsion; a year after His arrival, when the Greatest Holy Leaf was eight, He withdrew for two years to the mountains of Sulaymáníyyih, living as a dervish, His whereabouts unknown to His family and admirers alike. This sacrifice, however, did not avert calamity; the internal and external enemies of His Faith had relentlessly pursued their ends, and in May 1863, just after Bahá'u'lláh had revealed His own station to some of His followers, for the second time Bahíyyih Khánum became an exile and travelled with her mother and other women in covered carts for almost four months from Baghdád to Constantinople, the capital of the Ottoman Empire, in the caravan of her Father, which comprised about seventy of His followers. By now the young girl had turned her back on the world—a decision which is ever an inward orienta-tion—and was wholly dedicated, every moment of

her life, to serving her Divine Father, her Brother
'Abdu'l-Bahá Whom she adored, her frail, heroic
and beloved mother, her younger brother Mihdí
who had rejoined them, and all the followers of
Bahá'u'lláh—indeed, all and sundry who ever
crossed her path!

Yet a third banishment lay ahead of the Greatest Holy
Leaf; with no warning or justification, four months
after their arrival, in the depths of a very bitter
winter, the Sulṭán once again exiled Bahá'u'lláh, His
family and companions, this time to the city of his
displeasure, Adrianople. At the beginning of
December, for twelve days, over the wind-swept
plains of western Turkey, in storms of snow and rain,
in carts and on pack animals, the party struggled,
Bahá'u'lláh Himself testifying that *'Neither My
family, nor those who accompanied Me, had the necessary
raiment to protect them from the cold in that freezing
weather.'* 'Abdu'l-Bahá, Who rode beside His
Father's conveyance, was again badly frost-bitten, as
He had already been on the long journey from
Ṭihrán to Baghdád, and suffered its effects till the
end of His life. On their arrival, ill, destitute,
prisoners, they were assigned to crowded, cold,
vermin-infested houses—for Bahíyyih Khánum
the most repugnant of all her sufferings. So terrible
was their plight during this period that Bahá'u'lláh
asserts: *'The eyes of Our enemies wept over Us, and
beyond them those of every discerning person.'*

During the four years and eight months they sojourned in Adrianople fresh horrors attended the exiled family. In spite of Bahá'u'lláh's every effort to redeem His half-brother, Mírzá Yaḥyá, his intense jealousy reached its apex and he poisoned Bahá'u'lláh, Whose life hung in the balance for a month, and Who carried the mark of this treachery in a trembling hand until the end of His life.

The Greatest Holy Leaf often stated that all the years of her life, from childhood to maturity, were overshadowed by the constant threat that she might be separated from her beloved Father; it was a very real threat for on a number of occasions there was a plan to divide the exiles, Bahá'u'lláh to be sent to some unknown destination and His family to another. Once again the machinations of His enemies, within and without, ripened into a plan of this nature. The same Sulṭán who had exiled Him from Baghdád to Constantinople, and from Constantinople to Adrianople, now issued another edict of exile which was to carry Him to the prison-city of 'Akká in Syria for the last twenty-four years of His life—but His frantic family did not know this, they only knew another exile, and probably permanent separation, now lay ahead.

After a miserable, crowded voyage of ten days, with little food, through rough seas, in August heat, the band of exiles—still all together due to the masterful intervention of 'Abdu'l-Bahá—were finally locked into the barracks of the prison-city of 'Akká. Illness, death, privation were their lot for two years, the worst blow of all being the death of the gentle, universally loved Mihdí who, while walking on the prison roof and meditating, fell through an opening and died of his injuries. His body was washed in the presence of his Father Whose poignant grief has been recorded by Him; what went on in the hearts of the tender mother, the loving sister, we can only imagine.

Slowly the wheels of destiny revolved. Through the unceasing efforts of 'Abdu'l-Bahá, Bahá'u'-lláh was able, although still a prisoner, to live the last years of His life in relative peace in a beautiful mansion in the countryside outside 'Akká. Bahíyyih Khánum, however, continued to live in 'Akká with 'Abdu'l-Bahá and His family, whose imprisonment was not permanently lifted until the fall of the Sultánate in 1908 freed all political prisoners. The sun of the glory of her Father set in 1892, an event which again led to violent upheavals caused by internal and external enemies of the Faith; but the selfless devotion, the consecration to service in whatever form was needed, which had been manifested in Bahíyyih Khánum's life since she was six years old, continued unchanged; her whole being now revolved about the Brother she adored, the Centre of His Father's Covenant, the Head of His Faith. During the years of ever-increasing freedom and victory 'Abdu'l-Bahá embarked upon His history-making visits to Egypt, Europe and North America. Some of His letters to the Greatest Holy Leaf reflect not only His constant love and thoughts of her but His joy over the triumphant nature of His tour. But once again, inevitably it seems in her sorrow-filled life, great afflictions came upon her. In November 1921 this Brother—so adored, so close a companion since their earliest childhood—closed His eyes and passed away from a world that had so honoured Him, so afflicted Him for almost four score years.

The death of the partner in her trials, her exiles, her family's upheavals and crises, would have been sufficient for any woman of her age; added to it now came the condition of 'Abdu'l-Bahá's successor, His eldest grandson, appointed Guardian of His Faith, a young man of twenty-four, devastated with grief because 'Abdu'l-Bahá had died during his absence at Oxford University, and completely overwhelmed and prostrated by the news of the station and responsibilities conferred upon him in his Grandfather's Will and Testament. As always Bahíyyih Khánum rose to the occasion, comforted, supported, nursed and encouraged the heartbroken youth, the youth of whom, when he was a child, 'Abdu'l-Bahá had written to her: '*Kiss the fresh flower of the garden of sweetness, Shoghi Effendi.*' More than this, she accepted the headship of the

Faith which Shoghi Effendi, in his great distress, conferred upon her when he withdrew, as he wrote, until such time as '. . . having gained health, strength, self-confidence and spiritual energy' he would be able to take into his hands 'entirely and regularly the work of service. . .'. Upon Bahíyyih K͟hánum's frail shoulders yet again God placed a heavy load. Though she was now seventy-five, she bore, with her usual nobility, dignity, self-efface-ment and great inner assurance and strength, all the terrible events related to and produced by the ascension of her Brother. At last came the great freeing, her turn to shake the dust of this earth from her feet and wing away to realms on high. But the release and reward for her was far different for him whom she left behind; 'to one who was reared by the hands of her loving kindness', Shoghi Effendi wrote, 'the burden of this direst of calamities is well-nigh unbearable'. Torrents of passionate feel-ing poured from his pen, in English to the Bahá'ís of the West, in Persian and Arabic to the Bahá'ís of the East. All his love and, above all, her glory, became embodied in immortal words. During the 36 years of the Guardian's ministry he never ceased to remember her, to associate her with the unfold-ment of the Faith throughout the world, the rise of its institutions at the World Centre, the largest or smallest of his own undertakings; whether publicly or quietly in his personal life, her memory and influence were always there. He summed up what she represented historically, and to him personally in his dedication to her of *The Dawn Breakers*—the masterpiece he created out of Nabil's Narrative through his unique translation:

To
The Greatest Holy Leaf
The Last Survivor of a Glorious and Heroic Age
I Dedicate This Work
in Token of a
Great Debt of Gratitude and Love

Haifa
February 1982.

I

From the Writings of
BAHÁ'U'LLÁH

I

From the Writings of
BAHÁ'U'LLÁH

1. LET these exalted words be thy love-song on the tree of Bahá, O thou most holy and resplendent Leaf: 'God, besides Whom is none other God, the Lord of this world and the next!' Verily, We have elevated thee to the rank of one of the most distinguished among thy sex, and granted thee, in My court, a station such as none other woman hath surpassed. Thus have We preferred thee and raised thee above the rest, as a sign of grace from Him Who is the Lord of the throne on high and earth below. We have created thine eyes to behold the light of My countenance, thine ears to hearken unto the melody of My words, thy body to pay homage before My throne. Do thou render thanks unto God, thy Lord, the Lord of all the world.

How high is the testimony of the Sadratu'l-Muntahá for its leaf; how exalted the witness of the Tree of Life unto its fruit! Through My remembrance of her a fragrance laden with the perfume of musk hath been diffused; well is it with him that hath inhaled it and exclaimed: 'All praise be to Thee, O God, my

Lord the most glorious!' How sweet thy presence before Me; how sweet to gaze upon thy face, to bestow upon thee My loving-kindness, to favour thee with My tender care, to make mention of thee in this, My Tablet—a Tablet which I have ordained as a token of My hidden and manifest grace unto thee.

2.   O MY Leaf! Hearken thou unto My Voice: Verily there is none other God but Me, the Almighty, the All-Wise. I can well inhale from thee the fragrance of My love and the sweet-smelling savour wafting from the raiment of My Name, the Most Holy, the Most Luminous. Be astir upon God's Tree in conformity with thy pleasure and unloose thy tongue in praise of thy Lord amidst all mankind. Let not the things of the world grieve thee. Cling fast unto this divine Lote-Tree from which God hath graciously caused thee to spring forth. I swear by My life! It behoveth the lover to be closely joined to the loved one, and here indeed is the Best-Beloved of the world.

II

From the Writings of
'ABDU'L-BAHÁ

II

From the Writings of
'ABDU'L-BAHÁ

1. O MY well-beloved, deeply spiritual sister! Day and night thou livest in my memory. Whenever I remember thee my heart swelleth with sadness and my regret groweth more intense. Grieve not, for I am thy true, thy unfailing comforter. Let neither despondency nor despair becloud the serenity of thy life or restrain thy freedom. These days shall pass away. We will, please God, in the Abhá Kingdom and beneath the sheltering shadow of the Blessed Beauty, forget all these our earthly cares and will find each one of these base calumnies amply compensated by His expressions of praise and favour. From the beginning of time sorrow and anxiety, regret and tribulation, have always been the lot of every loyal servant of God. Ponder this in thine heart and consider how very true it is. Wherefore, set thine heart on the tender mercies of the Ancient Beauty and be thou filled with abiding joy and intense gladness. . . .

2. O THOU my affectionate sister! In the day-time and in the night-season my thoughts ever turn to thee. Not for one moment do I cease to remember thee. My sorrow and regret concern not myself; they centre around thee. Whenever I recall thine afflictions, tears that I cannot repress rain down from mine eyes. . . .

3.   DEAR and deeply spiritual sister! At morn and eventide, with the utmost ardour and humility, I supplicate at the Divine Threshold, and offer this, my prayer:

'Grant, O Thou my God, the Compassionate, that that pure and blessed Leaf may be comforted by Thy sweet savours of holiness and sustained by the reviving breeze of Thy loving care and mercy. Reinforce her spirit with the signs of Thy King-dom, and gladden her soul with the testimonies of Thy everlasting dominion. Comfort, O my God, her sorrowful heart with the remembrance of Thy face, initiate her into Thy hidden mysteries, and inspire her with the revealed splendours of Thy heavenly light. Manifold are her sorrows, and infinitely grievous her distress. Bestow con-tinually upon her the favour of Thy sustaining grace and, with every fleeting breath, grant her the blessing of Thy bounty. Her hopes and expectations are centred in Thee; open Thou to her face the portals of Thy tender mercies and lead her into the ways of Thy wondrous benevolence.

Thou art the Generous, the All-Loving, the Sustainer, the All-Bountiful. . . .'

4. DEAR sister, beloved of my heart and soul! The news of thy safe arrival and pleasant stay in the land of Egypt has reached me and filled my heart with exceeding gladness. I am thankful to Bahá'u'lláh for the good health thou dost enjoy and for the happiness He hath imparted to the hearts of the loved ones in that land. Shouldst thou wish to know of the condition of this servant of the Threshold of the Abhá Beauty, praise be to Him for having enabled me to inhale the fragrance of His tender mercy and partake of the delights of His loving-kindness and blessings. I am being continually reinforced by the energizing rays of His grace, and feel upheld by the uninterrupted aid of the victorious hosts of His Kingdom. My physical health is also improving. God be praised that from every quarter I receive the glad-tidings of the growing ascendancy of the Cause of God, and can witness evidences of the increasing influence of its spread. . . .

5. O THOU my loving, my deeply spiritual sister! I trust that by the grace and loving-kindness of the one true God thou art, and wilt be, kept safe and secure beneath the sheltering shadow of the Blessed Beauty. Night and day thy countenance

appeareth before mine eyes, and in my mind are
engraved the traits of thy character. . . .

6.   To MY honoured and distinguished sister do
thou convey the expression of my heartfelt, my
intense longing. Day and night she liveth in my
remembrance. I dare make no mention of the
feelings which separation from her has aroused in
mine heart; for whatever I should attempt to
express in writing will assuredly be effaced by the
tears which such sentiments must bring to mine
eyes. . . .

7.   O Ḍíyá![1] It is incumbent upon thee,
throughout the journey, to be a close, a constant
and cheerful companion to my honoured and distinguished sister. Unceasingly, with the utmost
vigour and devotion, exert thyself, by day and
night, to gladden her blessed heart; for all her days
she was denied a moment of tranquillity. She was
astir and restless every hour of her life. Moth-like
she circled in adoration round the undying flame of
the Divine Candle, her spirit ablaze and her heart
consumed by the fire of His love. . . .

8.   O THOU my affectionate sister!
God be praised, according to what we hear the

[1] Daughter of 'Abdu'l-Bahá.

climate in that land hath proved not unfavourable. It is to be hoped that out of the grace of the Blessed Beauty thy illness will be completely cured and thou wilt return in the best of health, so that once again I may gaze upon that wondrous face of thine.

Write thou a full account of thy condition by every post, for I am most anxious for news of thee. Let me know if thou shouldst desire anyone from here to come to thee, that I may send the person along—even Munírih—so that thou wilt not be homesick.

That thou shouldst spend a few days of peace and rest, is my dearest wish.

We here, God be thanked, are all enjoying the best of health. I have been better lately, and sleeping well at night. Rest assured.

9. O MY dear sister!

Praise be to God, within the sheltering grace of the Blessed Beauty, here in the lands of the West a breeze hath blown from over the rose-gardens of His bestowals, and the hearts of many people have been drawn as by a magnet to the Abhá Realm.

Whatever hath come to pass is from the confirmations of the Beloved; for otherwise, what merit had we, or what capacity? We are as a helpless babe, but fed at the breast of heavenly grace. We are no more than weak plants, but we flourish in the spring rain of His bestowals.

Wherefore, as a thank-offering for these bounties, on a certain day don thy garb to visit the Shrine, the ka'bih of our heart's desire, turn thyself toward Him on my behalf, lay down thy head on that sacred Threshold, and say:

O divine Providence! O Thou forgiving Lord! Sinner though I be, I have no refuge save Thyself. All praise be Thine, that in my wanderings over mountains and plains, my toils and troubles on the seas, Thou hast answered still my cries for help, and confirmed me, and favoured me, and honoured me with service at Thy Threshold.

To a feeble ant, Thou hast given Solomon's might. Thou hast made of a gnat a lion in the thicket of Thy Mercy. Thou hast bestowed on a drop the swelling waves of the sea, Thou hast carried up a mote to the pinnacles of grace. Whatever was achieved, was made possible through Thee. Otherwise, what strength did the fragile dust possess, what power did this feeble being have?

O divine Providence! Do not seize us in our sins, but give us refuge. Do not look upon our evil ways, but grant forgiveness. Consider not our just deserts, but open wide Thy door of grace.

Thou art the Mighty, the Powerful! Thou art the Seer, the Knower!

10. O MY well-beloved sister, O Most Exalted Leaf!

Thou didst leave for 'Akká to remain but two days or so and then return, but now thou hast been gone from us for quite a while. We have stayed behind in Haifa, all alone, and it is very difficult to get along. We hear that thou art a little indisposed; the Haifa air would have been better for thee. We had everything ready in Haifa to receive thee, but in fact, this caused thee some difficulty. There is no way but to endure the toil and trouble of God's path. If thou dost not bear these hardships, who would ever bear them?

In any case, no matter how things are, come thou here today, because my heart is longing for thee.

11. O THOU my sister, my dear sister!

Divine wisdom hath decreed this temporary separation, but I long more and more to be with thee again. Patience is called for, and long-suffering, and trust in God, and the seeking of His favour. Since thou art there, my mind is completely at rest.

In recent days, I have made a plan to visit Egypt, if this be God's will. Do thou, on my behalf, lay thy head on the sacred Threshold, and perfume brow and hair in the dust of that Door, and ask that I may be confirmed in my work; that I may, in return for His endless bounties, win, if He will, a drop out of the ocean of servitude.

12. MY SISTER and beloved of my soul!

Here on the slopes of Mount Carmel, by the cave

of Elijah, we are thinking of that Most Exalted Leaf, and the beloved and handmaids of the Lord.

We pass our days in writing and our nights now in communion with God, now in bed to overcome failing health. And although, to outward seeming, we are absent from you all, and far away, still our thoughts are with you always.

I can never, never forget thee. However great the distance that separates us, we still feel as though we were seated under the same roof, in one and the same gathering, for are we not all under the shadow of the Tabernacle of God and beneath the canopy of His infinite grace and mercy?

13. MY SISTER, for a considerable period, that is, from the day of Bahá'u'lláh's ascension, had grown so thin and feeble, and was in such a weakened condition from the anguish of her mourning, that she was close to breakdown.

Although, so far as she was concerned, it was her dearest wish to drain her cup and wing her way to the realms where the Divine Essence shineth in glory, still this servant could not bear to behold her in that state. Then it occurred to me that, God be thanked, I have such an unfailing comforter as Jináb-i-Hájí,[1] and it would be well to make him my partner in distress. I therefore determined to

[1] Hájí Mírzá Hasan-i-Khurásání (see H. M. Balyuzi, *'Abdu'l-Bahá*, pp. 86, 124).

send her to Egypt, to provide her with a change of air.

Although this will certainly cause thee trouble and inconvenience, still, I trust that out of God's bounty, it will also bring thee much joy and good cheer.

14.   O MY spiritual sister!

Thou didst go away to Haifa, supposedly for only three or four days. Now it becometh apparent that the spiritual power of the Shrine hath brought thee joy and radiance, and even as a magnet is holding thee fast. Thou surely wouldst remember us as well.

Truly the spiritual quality of the holy place, its fresh skies and delicate air, its crystal waters and sweet plains and charming seascape, and the holy breathings from the Kingdom all do mingle in that Sacred Fold. Thou art right to linger there . . .

Kiss the light of the eyes of the company of spiritual souls, Shoghi Effendi . . .

15.   O MY spiritual sister!

God be praised, through the Ancient Beauty's grace and bounty, we have set foot safe and sound upon this shore, and arrived in this town[1] . . .

These coasts were once the place where the breezes of God's loving kindness blew, and here in this sacred Vale the Son of Spirit[2] raised up His call

[1] Tiberias.   [2] Jesus.

of 'Here am I, O Thou My Lord! Here am I!' That is why we here perceive, from every direction, the sweet breathings of holiness.

My meaning is, rest thou assured, this servant is suffering neither from any trouble, nor hardship, nor fatigue. I am looking after myself, and keeping away from all mental preoccupations; all, that is, except for one thought, which doth indeed disquiet the mind—and that is, God forbid, that thou shouldst sorrow.

I hope that out of the bestowals and bounties of the Ancient Beauty, He will in His grace bring comfort to every heart.

16.   O MY affectionate sister!
God be praised, through His grace and favour, my health and well-being are now restored, but it is very hard for me to bear thine absence.

We think of thee at all times, here on the slopes of this sacred, holy and blessed Mount Carmel, and we are being happy on thy behalf . . .

17.   O MY dear sister!
It is quite a while now, since thou hast left us, and gone away to Nazareth and Haifa. This journey hath lasted too long. The weather in 'Akká is fine and

moderate. If thou comest back, it will rejoice our hearts. . . .

18. O MY cherished sister!

Thou art never absent from my thoughts.

I speak of thee and call thee to mind at all times. It is my hope that out of God's favour and grace thou dost keep safe and well, and dost visit the two Sacred Thresholds on my behalf.

19. O MY sister in the spirit, and the companion of my heart!

God willing, the climate of Haifa hath proved favourable. I hope that out of the bounties of the Ancient Beauty thou wilt gain a measure of peace and health.

I bring thee to mind both night and day. Just recently I had hoped to come to Haifa to visit thee, but various problems and the pressure of work have left me no time; for I want to see the travellers off, and every one of them presented a long list of names. God be thanked, I have written to them all.

Kiss the fresh flower of the garden of sweetness, Shoghi Effendi.

20. O THOU Greatest and Most Merciful Holy Leaf!

I arrived in New York in the best of health, and I

have been at all times thinking of thee, and sup-
plicating fervently at the threshold of the Blessed
Beauty that He may guard thee in the stronghold of
His protection. We are in the utmost fellowship and
joy. I hope that thou wilt be sheltered under His
bountiful care.

Write to me at once about Rúḥá Khánum's and
Shoghi Effendi's condition, informing me fully and
hiding nothing; this is the best way.

Convey my utmost longing to all.

21. I DO not know in what words I could
describe my longing for my honoured sister. Whatever it may write, my pen falls short.

III

From the Writings of
SHOGHI EFFENDI

III

From the Writings of
SHOGHI EFFENDI

1. THIS servant, after that grievous event and great calamity, the ascension of His Holiness 'Abdu'l-Bahá to the Abhá Kingdom, has been so stricken with grief and pain and so entangled in the troubles created by the enemies of the Cause of God, that I consider that my presence here, at such a time and in such an atmosphere, is not in accordance with the fulfilment of my important and sacred duties.

For this reason, unable to do otherwise, I have left for a time the affairs of the Cause both at home and abroad, under the supervision of the Holy Family and the headship of the Greatest Holy Leaf until, by the Grace of God, having gained health, strength, self-confidence and spiritual energy, and having taken into my hands, in accordance with my aim and desire, entirely and regularly the work of service I shall attain to my utmost spiritual hope and aspiration.

2. AND in this fervent plea, my voice is once more reinforced by the passionate, and perhaps, the

last, entreaty, of the Greatest Holy Leaf, whose
spirit, now hovering on the edge of the Great
Beyond, longs to carry on its flight to the Abhá
Kingdom, and into the presence of a Divine, an
almighty Father, an assurance of the joyous consummation of an enterprise,[1] the progress of which
has so greatly brightened the closing days of her
earthly life.

3. GREATEST HOLY LEAF'S IMMORTAL SPIRIT
WINGED ITS FLIGHT GREAT BEYOND. COUNTLESS LOVERS
HER SAINTLY LIFE IN EAST AND WEST SEIZED WITH
PANGS OF ANGUISH, PLUNGED IN UNUTTERABLE
SORROW. HUMANITY SHALL ERELONG RECOGNIZE ITS
IRREPARABLE LOSS. OUR BELOVED FAITH, WELL-NIGH
CRUSHED BY DEVASTATING BLOW OF 'ABDU'L-BAHÁ'S
UNEXPECTED ASCENSION, NOW LAMENTS PASSING LAST
REMNANT OF BAHÁ'U'LLÁH, ITS MOST EXALTED
MEMBER. HOLY FAMILY CRUELLY DIVESTED ITS MOST
PRECIOUS, MOST GREAT ADORNING. I, FOR MY PART,
BEWAIL SUDDEN REMOVAL MY SOLE EARTHLY SUS-
TAINER, THE JOY AND SOLACE OF MY LIFE. HER SACRED
REMAINS WILL REPOSE VICINITY HOLY SHRINES. SO
GRIEVOUS A BEREAVEMENT NECESSITATES SUSPENSION
FOR NINE MONTHS THROUGHOUT BAHÁ'Í WORLD EVERY
MANNER RELIGIOUS FESTIVITY. INFORM LOCAL ASSEMB-
LIES AND GROUPS HOLD BEFITTING MANNER MEMORIAL
GATHERINGS, EXTOL A LIFE SO LADEN SACRED EXPERI-
ENCES, SO RICH IMPERISHABLE MEMORIES . . . ADVISE

[1] Construction of the House of Worship in Wilmette, Illinois.

HOLDING ADDITIONAL COMMEMORATION SERVICE OF
STRICTLY DEVOTIONAL CHARACTER AUDITORIUM
MASHRIQU'L-ADHKÁR.

4. GREATEST HOLY LEAF ASCENDED ABHÁ KING-
DOM. OUR GRIEF IMMENSE, OUR LOSS IRREPARABLE.
INFORM LOCAL ASSEMBLIES COMMEMORATE BEFIT-
TINGLY SACRED EXPERIENCES SO RICH, SO SUBLIME, SO
EVENTFUL A LIFE. MAGNITUDE OF OUR SORROW
DEMANDS COMPLETE SUSPENSION FOR NINE MONTHS
THROUGHOUT BAHÁ'Í WORLD EVERY FORM RELIGIOUS
FESTIVITY. HER MORTAL REMAINS LAID VICINITY HOLY
SHRINE.

5. O YE who burn in the flames of bereavement!
By the Day-star of the World, my bereaved and
longing heart is afire with a grief that is beyond my
description. The sudden, the grievous and calamitous news that the Most Exalted, the pure, the holy,
the immaculate, the brightly shining Leaf, the
Remnant of Bahá, and His trust, the eternal fruit
and the one last remembrance of the Holy Tree
—may my life be offered for the wrongs she
suffered—has ascended, reached me like live coals
cast into a frail and afflicted heart. The foundations
of my serenity were shattered, and tears of desolation came like a flood that carries all away.

Alas, that I was prevented from being with her at
the close of her earthly days, at that moment when

she ascended to her Lord, her Master, and when her delicate body was placed in the tomb. Not mine that honour, that high privilege, for I was far away, deprived, bereft, excluded.

O brothers and sisters in the spirit! In this solemn hour, from one direction we can hear the sounds of loud weeping, and cries of mourning and woe, rising out of the throats of the people of Bahá throughout this nether world, because of their separation from that rich mine of faithfulness, that Orb of the heaven of eternal glory—because of her setting below the horizon of this holy Spot. But from another direction can be heard the songs of praise and holy exultation from the Company on High and the undying dwellers in Paradise, and from beyond them all God's Prophets, coming forth to welcome that fair being, and to place her in the retreats of glory, and to seat her at the right hand of Him Who is the Centre of God's Mighty Covenant.

The community of Bahá, whether in the East of the world or the West, are lamenting like orphans left destitute; fevered, tormented, unquiet, they are voicing their grief. Out of the depths of their sorrowing hearts, there rises to the Abhá Horizon this continual piercing cry: 'Where art thou gone, O torch of tender love? Where art thou gone, O source of grace and mercy? Where art thou gone, O symbol of bounty and generosity? Where art thou gone, O day-spring of detachment in this world of being? Where art thou gone, O trust left by Bahá among His people, O remnant left by Him among

His servants, O sweet scent of His garment, shed across all created things!'

O ye who loved that luminous face! The oil within that shining lamp was used up in this world and its light was extinguished; and yet, in the lamp-niche of the Kingdom, the fingers of the Lord of the heavenly throne have kindled it so bright, and it has cast such a splendour on the maids of Heaven—dwelling in chambers of red rubies and circling about her—that they all called from out their souls and hearts, 'O joy upon joy!' and with shouts of, 'Well done! Well done! Upon thee be God's blessings, O Most Exalted Leaf!' did they welcome that quintessence of love and purity within the towering pavilions of eternity.

At that time, as bidden by the Lord, the Protector, the Self-Subsisting, did the heavenly Crier raise up his voice and cry out: 'O Most Exalted Leaf! Thou art she who did endure with patience in God's way from thine earliest childhood and throughout all thy life, and did bear in His pathway what none other hath borne, save only God in His own Self, the Supreme Ruler over all created things, and before Him, His noble Herald, and after Him, His holy Branch, the One, the Inaccessible, the Most High. The people of the Concourse on High seek the fragrance of thy presence, and the dwellers in the retreats of eternity circle about thee. To this bear witness the souls of the cherubim within the tabernacles of majesty and might, and beyond them the tongue of God the One True Lord, the Pure, the

Most Wondrous. Blessedness be thine and a goodly abode; glad tidings to thee and a happy ending!'

To one who was reared by the hands of her loving kindness, the burden of this direst of calamities is well nigh unbearable; and yet praised be the God of glory that her fragile frame has escaped from the prison of continual ordeals and afflictions which, with an astonishing forbearance, and for more than eighty years, she accepted and endured. Now is she free; delivered from her chains of care and sorrow; safe from all the suffering and pain, released from the ills of this nether world. She rolled up and packed away the years of longing for her mighty Father, and for Him, her loving and well-favoured Brother, and departed to her abode in the midmost heart of the Heavens.

This heavenly being, during all the turmoil of her days, did not rest for a moment, nor ever did she seek quiet and peace. From the beginning of her life, from her very childhood, she tasted sorrow's cup; she drank down the afflictions and calamities of the earliest years of the great Cause of God. In the tumult of the Year of Hín,[1] as a result of the sacking and plundering of her glorious Father's wealth and holdings, she learned the bitterness of destitution and want. Then she shared the imprisonment, the grief, the banishment of the Abhá Beauty, and in the storm which broke out in 'Iráq—because of the plotting and the treachery of the prime mover of

[1] The numerical value of the letters composing 'Hín' indicates 1268 A.H. or 1851–52 A.D.

mischief, the focal centre of hate—she bore, with complete resignation and acquiescence, uncounted ordeals. She forgot herself, did without her kin, turned aside from possessions, struck off at one blow the bonds of every worldly concern; and then, like a lovelorn moth, she circled day and night about the flame of the matchless Beauty of her Lord.

In the heaven of severance, she shone like the Morning Star, fair and bright, and through her character and all her ways, she shed upon kin and stranger, upon the learned, and the lowly, the radiance of Bahá'u'lláh's surpassing perfection. Because of the intense and deep-seated sorrows and the manifold oppressive trials that assailed her —never failing spring of grace that she was, essence of loving-kindness—in the Land of Mystery[1] her lovely form was worn away to a breath, to a shadow; and during the Most Great Convulsion, which in the years of 'Stress' made every heart to quake, she stood as a soaring pillar, immovable and fixed; and from the blasts of desolation that rose and blew, that Leaf of the eternal Lote-Tree did not wither.

Rather did she redouble her efforts, urging herself on the more, to servitude and sacrifice. In captivating hearts and winning over souls, in destroying doubts and misgivings, she led the field. With the waters of her countless mercies, she brought thorny hearts to a blossoming of love from

[1] Adrianople.

the All-Glorious, and with the influence of her pure loving-kindness, transformed the implacable, the unyielding, into impassioned lovers of the celestial Beauty's peerless Cause.

Yet another wound was inflicted on her injured heart by the aggressions and violations of the evil-doers within the prison-fortress,[1] yet another blow was struck at her afflicted being. And then her anguish was increased by the passing of the Abhá Beauty, and the cruelty of the disloyal added more fuel to the fires of her mourning. In the midst of that storm of violation, the countenance of that rare treasure of the Lord shone all the brighter, and throughout the Bahá'í community, her value and high rank became clearly perceived. By the vehement onslaught of the chief of violators against the sacred beliefs of the followers of the Faith, she was neither frightened nor in despair.

In the days of the Commission of Investigation, she was a staunch and trusted supporter of the peerless Branch of Bahá'u'lláh, and a companion to Him beyond compare. At the time of His absence in the western world, she was His competent deputy, His representative and vicegerent, with none to equal her. In a Tablet from the pen of the Centre of the Covenant, addressed to His consort, are these words referring to His brilliant sister: 'To my honoured and distinguished sister do thou convey the expression of my heartfelt, my intense longing. Day and night she liveth in my remem-

[1] 'Akká.

Bahíyyih <u>Kh</u>ánum, *circa* 1895

Bahíyyih <u>Kh</u>ánum, 1919

Bahíyyih Khánum, *circa* 1931

Relics of the Greatest Holy Leaf preserved in the International Bahá'í Archives. The ring on the marble block at the left of the mirror is set with a stone bearing the symbol of the Greatest Name; the ring on the small tray, centre, is the seal of her own name, Bahíyyih.

brance. I dare make no mention of the feelings which separation from her has aroused in my heart, for whatever I should attempt to express in writing will assuredly be effaced by the tears which such sentiments must bring to my eyes.'

After the ascension of 'Abdu'l-Bahá to the realm of the All-Glorious, that Light of the Concourse on High enfolded me, helpless as I was, in the embrace of her love, and with incomparable pity and tenderness, persuaded, guided, and urged me on to the requirements of servitude. The very elements of this frail being were leavened with her love, refreshed by her companionship, sustained by her eternal spirit. Never for a moment will her kindnesses, her favours, pass from my memory, and as the months and the years go by, the effects of them on this mourning heart will never be diminished.

> *O Liege Lady of the people of Bahá!*
> *Broken is our circle by thy going—*
> *Broken our circle, broken too, our hearts.*

That my tongue, my pen could thank thee were a hopeless task, nor can any praise of mine befit thine excellence. Not even a droplet of all thine endless love can I aspire to fathom, nor can I adequately praise and tell of even the most trifling out of all the events of thy precious life. In the courts of the Almighty, for this frail being thy sacred spirit intercedeth, and in this darksome world, the sweet memory of thee is the succourer and friend of this lowly one. Thy comely face is etched for ever on the tablet of my grieving soul, those smiles that refreshed my life are forever and safely imprinted in the innermost recesses of my stricken heart. Let me not be forgotten by thee in the glorious precincts on high; leave me not despairing, nor excluded from the never-ceasing reinforcements that come from the living Lord; and in this world and the Kingdom, help me to reach what thou knowest to be my dearest hope.

O faithful friends! It is right and fitting that out of honour to her most high station, in the gatherings of the followers of Bahá'u'lláh, whether of the East or the West, all Bahá'í festivals and celebrations should be completely suspended for a period of nine months, and that in every city and village, memorial meetings should be held, with all solemnity, spirituality, lowliness and consecration—where, in the choicest of language, may be described at length the shining attributes of that most resplendent Leaf, that archetype of the people of Bahá. If it be possible for the individual believers to postpone their personal celebrations for a period of one year, let them unhesitatingly do so thus to express their sorrow at this agonizing misfortune. Let them read this letter, this supplication, in their memorial gatherings, that perchance the Almighty will lighten my burden, and dispel the clouds of my bereavement; that He will answer my prayers, and fulfil my hopes, out of His bounty, His power, His grace.

6. BRETHREN and fellow-mourners in the Faith of Bahá'u'lláh!

A sorrow, reminiscent in its poignancy, of the devastating grief caused by 'Abdu'l-Bahá's sudden removal from our midst, has stirred the Bahá'í world to its foundations. The Greatest Holy Leaf, the well-beloved and treasured Remnant of Bahá'u'lláh entrusted to our frail and unworthy hands by our departed Master, has passed to the Great Beyond, leaving a legacy that time can never dim.

The Community of the Most Great Name, in its entirety and to its very core, feels the sting of this cruel loss. Inevitable though this calamitous event appeared to us all, however acute our apprehensions of its steady approach, the consciousness of its final consummation at this terrible hour leaves us, we whose souls have been impregnated by the energizing influence of her love, prostrated and disconsolate.

How can my lonely pen, so utterly inadequate to glorify so exalted a station, so impotent to portray the experiences of so sublime a life, so disqualified to recount the blessings she showered upon me since my earliest childhood—how can such a pen repay the great debt of gratitude and love that I owe her whom I regarded as my chief sustainer, my most affectionate comforter, the joy and inspiration of my life? My grief is too immense, my remorse too profound, to be able to give full vent at this moment to the feelings that surge within me.

Only future generations and pens abler than mine can, and will, pay a worthy tribute to the towering grandeur of her spiritual life, to the unique part she played throughout the tumultuous stages of Bahá'í history, to the expressions of unqualified praise that have streamed from the pen of both Bahá'u'lláh and 'Abdu'l-Bahá, the Centre of His Covenant, though unrecorded, and in the main unsuspected by the mass of her passionate admirers in East and West, the share she has had in influencing the course of some of the chief events in the annals of the Faith, the sufferings she bore, the sacrifices she made, the rare gifts of unfailing sympathy she so strikingly displayed—these, and many others stand so inextricably interwoven with the fabric of the Cause itself that no future historian of the Faith of Bahá'u'lláh can afford to ignore or minimize.

As far back as the concluding stages of the heroic age of the Cause, which witnessed the imprisonment of Bahá'u'lláh in the Síyáh-C͟hál of Ṭihrán, the Greatest Holy Leaf, then still in her infancy, was privileged to taste of the cup of woe which the first believers of that Apostolic Age had quaffed.

How well I remember her recall, at a time when her faculties were still unimpaired, the gnawing suspense that ate into the hearts of those who watched by her side, at the threshold of her pillaged house, expectant to hear at any moment the news of Bahá'u'lláh's imminent execution! In those sinister hours, she often recounted, her parents had so

suddenly lost their earthly possessions that within
the space of a single day from being the privileged
member of one of the wealthiest families of Ṭihrán
she had sunk to the state of a sufferer from uncon-
cealed poverty. Deprived of the means of subsist-
ence her illustrious mother, the famed Navváb,
was constrained to place in the palm of her daughter's hand a handful of flour and to induce her to
accept it as a substitute for her daily bread.

And when at a later time this revered and precious
member of the Holy Family, then in her teens, came
to be entrusted by the guiding hand of her Father
with missions that no girl of her age could, or would
be willing to, perform, with what spontaneous joy
she seized her opportunity and acquitted herself of
the task with which she had been entrusted! The
delicacy and extreme gravity of such functions as
she, from time to time, was called upon to fulfil,
when the city of Baghdád was swept by the
hurricane which the heedlessness and perversity of
Mírzá Yaḥyá had unchained, as well as the tender
solicitude which, at so early an age, she evinced
during the period of Bahá'u'lláh's enforced retire-
ment to the mountains of Sulaymáníyyih, marked
her as one who was both capable of sharing the
burden, and willing to make the sacrifice, which her
high birth demanded.

How staunch was her faith, how calm her
demeanour, how forgiving her attitude, how severe
her trials, at a time when the forces of schism had
rent asunder the ties that united the little band of

exiles which had settled in Adrianople and whose fortunes seemed then to have sunk to their lowest ebb! It was in this period of extreme anxiety, when the rigours of a winter of exceptional severity, coupled with the privations entailed by unhealthy housing accommodation and dire financial distress, undermined once for all her health and sapped the vitality which she had hitherto so thoroughly enjoyed. The stress and storm of that period made an abiding impression upon her mind, and she retained till the time of her death on her beauteous and angelic face evidences of its intense hardships.

Not until, however, she had been confined in the company of Bahá'u'lláh within the walls of the prison-city of 'Akká did she display, in the plenitude of her power and in the full abundance of her love for Him, those gifts that single her out, next to 'Abdu'l-Bahá, among the members of the Holy Family, as the brightest embodiment of that love which is born of God and of that human sympathy which few mortals are capable of evincing.

Banishing from her mind and heart every earthly attachment, renouncing the very idea of matrimony, she, standing resolutely by the side of a Brother whom she was to aid and serve so well, arose to dedicate her life to the service of her Father's glorious Cause. Whether in the management of the affairs of His Household in which she excelled, or in the social relationships which she so assiduously cultivated in order to shield both Bahá'u'lláh and 'Abdu'l-Bahá, whether in the unfailing attention she paid to the everyday needs of her Father, or in the traits of generosity, of affability and kindness, which she manifested, the Greatest Holy Leaf had by that time abundantly demonstrated her worthiness to rank as one of the noblest figures intimately associated with the life-long work of Bahá'u'lláh.

How grievous was the ingratitude, how blind the fanaticism, how persistent the malignity of the officials, their wives, and their subordinates, in return for the manifold bounties which she, in close association with her Brother, so profusely conferred upon them! Her patience, her magnanimity, her undiscriminating benevolence, far from disarming the hostility of that perverse generation, served only to inflame their rancour, to excite their jealousy, to intensify their fears. The gloom that had settled upon that little band of imprisoned believers, who languished in the Fortress of 'Akká contrasted with the spirit of confident hope, of deep-rooted optimism that beamed upon her serene countenance. No calamity, however intense, could obscure the brightness of her saintly face, and no agitation, no matter how severe, could disturb the composure of her gracious and dignified behaviour.

That her sensitive heart instantaneously reacted to the slighest injury that befell the least significant of creatures, whether friend or foe, no one who knew her well could doubt. And yet such was the restraining power of her will—a will which her spirit of self-renunciation so often prompted her to suppress—that a superficial observer might well be led to question the intensity of her emotions or to belittle the range of her sympathies. In the school of adversity she, already endowed by Providence with the virtues of meekness and fortitude, learned through the example and exhortations of the Great Sufferer, Who was her Father, the lesson she was destined to teach the great mass of His followers for so long after Him.

Armed with the powers with which an intimate and long-standing companionship with Bahá'u'lláh had already equipped her, and benefiting by the magnificent example which the steadily widening range of 'Abdu'l-Bahá's activities afforded her, she was prepared to face the storm which the treacherous conduct of the Covenant-breakers had aroused and to withstand its most damaging onslaughts.

Great as had been her sufferings ever since her infancy, the anguish of mind and heart which the ascension of Bahá'u'lláh occasioned nerved her, as never before, to a resolve which no upheaval could bend and which her frail constitution belied. Amidst the dust and heat of the commotion which that faithless and rebellious company engendered she found herself constrained to dissolve ties of family relationship, to sever long-standing and intimate friendships, to discard lesser loyalties for the sake of her supreme allegiance to a Cause she had loved so dearly and had served so well.

The disruption that ensued found her ranged by the side of Him Whom her departed Father had appointed as the Centre of His Covenant and the authorized Expounder of His Word. Her venerated mother, as well as her distinguished paternal uncle, Áqáy-i-Kalím—the twin pillars who, all throughout the various stages of Bahá'u'lláh's exile from the Land of His Birth to the final place of His confinement, had demonstrated, unlike most of the members of His Family, the tenacity of their loyalty —had already passed behind the Veil. Death, in the most tragic circumstances, had also robbed her of the Purest Branch, her only brother besides 'Abdu'l-Bahá, while still in the prime of youth. She alone of the family of Bahá'u'lláh remained to cheer the heart and reinforce the efforts of the Most Great Branch, against Whom were solidly arrayed the almost entire company of His faithless relatives. In her arduous task she was seconded by the diligent efforts of Munírih Khánum, the Holy Mother, and those of her daughters whose age allowed them to assist in the accomplishment of that stupendous achievement with which the name of 'Abdu'l-Bahá will for ever remain associated.

With the passing of Bahá'u'lláh and the fierce onslaught of the forces of disruption that followed in its wake, the Greatest Holy Leaf, now in the hey-day of her life, rose to the height of her great opportunity and acquitted herself worthily of her task. It would take me beyond the compass of the tribute I am moved to pay to her memory were I to dwell upon the incessant machinations to which Muḥammad-'Alí, the arch-breaker of the Covenant of Bahá'u'lláh, and his despicable supporters basely resorted, upon the agitation which their cleverly-directed campaign of misrepresentation and calumny produced in quarters directly connected with Sulṭán 'Abdu'l-Ḥamíd and his advisers, upon the trials and investigations to which it gave rise, upon the rigidity of the incarceration it reimposed, and upon the perils it revived. Suffice it to say that but for her sleepless vigilance, her tact, her courtesy, her extreme patience and heroic fortitude, grave complications might have ensued and the load of 'Abdu'l-Bahá's anxious care would have been considerably increased.

And when the storm-cloud that had darkened the horizon of the Holy Land had been finally dissipated and the call raised by our beloved 'Abdu'l-Bahá had stirred to a new life certain cities of the American and European continents, the Most Exalted Leaf became the recipient of the unbounded affection and blessings of One Who could best estimate her virtues and appreciate her merits.

The decline of her precious life had by that time set in, and the burden of advancing age was beginning to becloud the radiance of her countenance. Forgetful of her own self, disdaining rest and comfort, and undeterred by the obstacles that still stood in her path, she, acting as the honoured hostess to a steadily increasing number of pilgrims who thronged 'Abdu'l-Bahá's residence from both the East and the West, continued to display those same attributes that had won her, in the preceding phases of her career, so great a measure of admiration and love.

And when, in pursuance of God's inscrutable Wisdom, the ban on 'Abdu'l-Bahá's confinement was lifted and the Plan which He, in the darkest hours of His confinement, had conceived materialized, He with unhesitating confidence, invested His trusted and honoured sister with the responsibility of attending to the multitudinous details arising out of His protracted absence from the Holy Land.

No sooner had 'Abdu'l-Bahá stepped upon the shores of the European and American continents than our beloved Khánum found herself well-nigh overwhelmed with thrilling messages, each betokening the irresistible advance of the Cause in a manner which, notwithstanding the vast range of her experience, seemed to her almost incredible. The years in which she basked in the sunshine of 'Abdu'l-Bahá's spiritual victories were, perhaps, among the brightest and happiest of her life. Little did she dream when, as a little girl, she was running about, in the courtyard of her Father's house in Tihrán, in the company of Him Whose destiny was to be one day the chosen Centre of God's indestructible Covenant, that such a Brother would be capable of achieving, in realms so distant, and among races so utterly remote, so great and memorable a victory.

The enthusiasm and joy which swelled in her breast as she greeted 'Abdu'l-Bahá on His triumphant return from the West, I will not venture to

describe. She was astounded at the vitality of which
He had, despite His unimaginable sufferings,
proved Himself capable. She was lost in admiration
at the magnitude of the forces which His utterances
had released. She was filled with thankfulness to
Bahá'u'lláh for having enabled her to witness the
evidences of such brilliant victory for His Cause no
less than for His Son.

The outbreak of the Great War gave her yet
another opportunity to reveal the true worth of her
character and to release the latent energies of her
heart. The residence of 'Abdu'l-Bahá in Haifa was
besieged, all throughout that dreary conflict, by a
concourse of famished men, women and children
whom the maladministration, the cruelty and neglect of the officials of the Ottoman Government had
driven to seek an alleviation to their woes. From the
hand of the Greatest Holy Leaf, and out of the
abundance of her heart, these hapless victims of a
contemptible tyranny, received day after day
unforgettable evidences of a love they had learned to
envy and admire. Her words of cheer and comfort,
the food, the money, the clothing she freely dispensed, the remedies which, by a process of her
own, she herself prepared and diligently applied
—all these had their share in comforting the disconsolate, in restoring sight to the blind, in sheltering
the orphan, in healing the sick, and in succouring the
homeless and the wanderer.

She had reached, amidst the darkness of the war

days the high water-mark of her spiritual attainments. Few, if any, among the unnumbered benefactors of society whose privilege has been to allay, in various measures, the hardships and sufferings entailed by that Fierce Conflict, gave as freely and as disinterestedly as she did; few exercised that undefinable influence upon the beneficiaries of their gifts.

Age seemed to have accentuated the tenderness of her loving heart, and to have widened still further the range of her sympathies. The sight of appalling suffering around her steeled her energies and revealed such potentialities that her most intimate associates had failed to suspect.

The ascension of 'Abdu'l-Bahá, so tragic in its suddenness, was to her a terrible blow from the effects of which she never completely recovered. To her He, Whom she called 'Áqá', had been a refuge in times of adversity. On Him she had been led to place her sole reliance. In Him she had found ample compensation for the bereavements she had suffered, the desertions she had witnessed, the ingratitude she had been shown by friends and kindred. No one could ever dream that a woman of her age, so frail in body, so sensitive of heart, so loaded with the cares of almost eighty years of incessant tribulation, could so long survive so shattering a blow. And yet, history, no less than the annals of our immortal Faith, shall record for her a share in the advancement and consolidation of the world-wide Community which the hand of 'Abdu'l-Bahá had helped to fashion, which no one among the remnants of His Family can rival.

Which of the blessings am I to recount, which in her unfailing solicitude she showered upon me, in the most critical and agitated hours of my life? To me, standing in so dire a need of the vitalizing grace of God, she was the living symbol of many an attribute I had learned to admire in 'Abdu'l-Bahá. She was to me a continual reminder of His inspiring personality, of His calm resignation, of His munificence and magnanimity. To me she was an incarnation of His winsome graciousness, of His all-encompassing tenderness and love.

It would take me too long to make even a brief allusion to those incidents of her life, each of which eloquently proclaims her as a daughter, worthy to inherit that priceless heritage bequeathed to her by Bahá'u'lláh. A purity of life that reflected itself in even the minutest details of her daily occupations and activities; a tenderness of heart that obliterated every distinction of creed, class and colour; a resignation and serenity that evoked to the mind the calm and heroic fortitude of the Báb; a natural fondness of flowers and children that was so characteristic of Bahá'u'lláh; an unaffected simplicity of manners; an extreme sociability which made her accessible to all; a generosity, a love, at once disinterested and undiscriminating, that reflected so clearly the attributes of 'Abdu'l-Bahá's character; a sweetness of temper; a cheerfulness that no amount of sorrow could becloud; a quiet and unassuming disposition that served to enhance a thousandfold the prestige of her exalted rank; a forgiving nature that instantly disarmed the most unyielding enemy —these rank among the outstanding attributes of a saintly life which history will acknowledge as having been endowed with a celestial potency that few of the heroes of the past possessed.

No wonder that in Tablets, which stand as eternal testimonies to the beauty of her character, Bahá'u'lláh and 'Abdu'l-Bahá have paid touching tributes to those things that testify to her exalted position among the members of their Family, that proclaim her as an example to their followers, and as an object worthy of the admiration of all mankind.

I need only, at this juncture, quote the following passage from a Tablet addressed by 'Abdu'l-Bahá to the Holy Mother, the tone of which reveals unmistakably the character of those ties that bound Him to so precious, so devoted a sister:

'*To my honoured and distinguished sister do thou convey the expression of my heartfelt, my intense longing. Day and night she liveth in my remembrance. I dare make no mention of the feelings which separation from her has aroused in my heart, for whatever I should attempt to express in writing will assuredly be effaced by the tears which such sentiments must bring to my eyes.*'

Dearly-beloved Greatest Holy Leaf! Through the mist of tears that fill my eyes I can clearly see, as I pen these lines, thy noble figure before me, and can recognize the serenity of thy kindly face. I can still gaze, though the shadows of the grave separate us, into thy blue, love-deep eyes, and can feel in its calm intensity, the immense love thou didst bear for the Cause of thine Almighty Father, the attachment that bound thee to the most lowly and insignificant among its followers, the warm affection thou didst cherish for me in thine heart. The memory of the ineffable beauty of thy smile shall ever continue to cheer and hearten me in the thorny path I am destined to pursue. The remembrance of the touch of thine hand shall spur me on to follow steadfastly in thy way. The sweet magic of thy voice shall remind me, when the hour of adversity is at its darkest, to hold fast to the rope thou didst seize so firmly all the days of thy life.

Bear thou this my message to 'Abdu'l-Bahá, thine exalted and divinely-appointed Brother: If the Cause for which Bahá'u'lláh toiled and laboured, for which Thou didst suffer years of agonizing sorrow, for the sake of which streams of sacred blood have flowed, should, in the days to come, encounter storms more severe than those it has already weathered, do Thou continue to overshadow, with Thine all-encompassing care and wisdom, Thy frail, Thy unworthy appointed child.

Intercede, O noble and well-favoured scion of a heavenly Father, for me no less than for the toiling masses of thy ardent lovers, who have sworn undying allegiance to thy memory, whose souls have been nourished by the energies of thy love, whose conduct has been moulded by the inspiring example of thy life, and whose imaginations are fired by the imperishable evidences of thy lively faith, thy unshakable constancy, thy invincible heroism, thy great renunciation.

Whatever betide us, however distressing the vicissitudes which the nascent Faith of God may yet experience, we pledge ourselves, before the mercy-seat of thy glorious Father, to hand on, unimpaired and undivided, to generations yet unborn, the glory of that tradition of which thou hast been its most brilliant exemplar.

In the innermost recesses of our hearts, O thou exalted Leaf of the Abhá Paradise, we have reared for thee a shining mansion that the hand of time can never undermine, a shrine which shall frame eternally the matchless beauty of thy countenance, an altar whereon the fire of thy consuming love shall burn for ever.

7. ENTREAT SORROW STRICKEN AMERICAN BELIEVERS NEVER ALLOW CONSCIOUSNESS THEIR AGONIZING LOSS PARALYZE DETERMINATION PROSECUTE AN ENTERPRISE ON WHICH ADORED OBJECT OUR MOURNING CENTRED HER BRIGHTEST HOPES.

8. YOUR MESSAGE ALLEVIATED LOAD MY AGONIZING SORROW. NOTHING LESS INFLEXIBLE RESOLVE CARRY OUT HER DEAREST PARTING WISH HOLD FAST CAUSE HER ALMIGHTY FATHER CAN LIFT ITS CRUSHING BURDEN.

9. PRAY ASSURE AMERICAN BELIEVERS BEHALF HOLY
FAMILY MYSELF ABIDING APPRECIATION NUMEROUS
EVIDENCES THEIR VALUED SYMPATHY. OUR SORROW-
LADEN HEARTS MUCH RELIEVED FILLED WITH GRATI-
TUDE. OUT OF PANGS OF ANGUISH WHICH BEREAVED
AMERICA EXPERIENCED IN HER SUDDEN SEPARATION
FROM 'ABDU'L-BAHÁ ADMINISTRATION GOD'S MIGHTY
FAITH WAS BORN. MIGHT NOT HER PRESENT GRIEF AT
LOSS BAHÁ'U'LLÁH'S PRECIOUS DAUGHTER RELEASE
SUCH FORCES AS WILL ENSURE SPEEDY COMPLETION
MASHRIQU'L-ADHKÁR THE ADMINISTRATION'S MIGHTY
BULWARK, SYMBOL OF ITS STRENGTH AND HARBINGER
ITS PROMISED GLORY.

10. YOUR valued message brought strength and
solace to my aching heart. I deeply appreciate the
sentiments of my invaluable fellow-workers, who
have by their eminent, their unforgettable and
unique services, contributed so powerfully in
brightening the closing days of her precious life. The
services each of you has rendered to our beloved
Cause brought much joy and hope to her in the
evening of her life, and are, therefore, highly
meritorious in the sight of the Almighty. May He
bless abundantly your work in the Divine Vineyard,
and enable you to render still greater services in the
days to come.

11. I DEEPLY appreciate your sympathy. My loss
is tremendous and my sorrow so profound. I will

pray that you, who have felt the power of her spirit at so advanced an age may be enabled to mirror forth its splendour and reveal its beauty to the world. I will continue to pray in your behalf. You are often in my thoughts. Rest assured and persevere in your devoted efforts.

12. I GREATLY value your sympathy in my cruel, my irreparable loss. My only comfort is the assurance of her devoted lovers to remain firm and steadfast in the Cause and to strive to follow in her footsteps. The example of her life is our solace, our inspiration and strength. May the Beloved aid you to follow in her way, and to perpetuate her glorious memory.

13. YOUR sweet and touching message imparted strength and solace to my heart. I value the sentiments you express and am deeply grateful. My grief is profound and my only comfort is the thought that her many lovers, East and West, are straining every nerve to promote those very ideals for which she suffered and toiled all the days of her eventful and sacred life. I will continue to pray for your welfare and success from the depths of my heart. Rest assured.

14. MY great love for the Greatest Holy Leaf and my attachment to each one of you prompt me to add these few words in person and to express to you my gratitude for the expression of your valued sympathy. I greatly value your message, and will pray that the Almighty may bless your efforts in the service of a Cause for the sake of which our loved Khánum sacrificed her precious life.

15. THE many evidences of your increasing zeal and activities in the service of our beloved Cause, have to a great measure, relieved my sorrow-laden heart. I will continue to pray for your unsparing efforts, and wish you to persevere, whatever the vicissitudes which this immortal Faith may encounter in future. Rest assured, and never feel disconsolate . . .

The celebration of Bahá'í festive anniversaries, I feel, should also be suspended during a period of nine months.

16. YOUR highly impressive and touching message brought much relief to my weary soul. I thank you from the depths of my heart. I greatly value the sentiments expressed on behalf of a local community, the members of which have, by their services, their devotion and loyalty, contributed, to so great an extent, to the joy and satisfaction of the hearts of both 'Abdu'l-Bahá and the Greatest Holy Leaf. My great attachment to each one of you, as well as my immense love for our departed and beloved <u>Kh</u>ánum, have prompted me to add these few words in person. I will continue to pray for the success of your efforts, as well as for your spiritual advancement.

17. THE passing of the Greatest Holy Leaf has filled my heart with unutterable sorrow. My comfort is the thought that the measure of success achieved, under your wise and able leadership, by the collective efforts of the American believers has brightened considerably the last days of her precious life. Would to God that the continued endeavours of this little band of her devoted lovers who have brought so great a joy to her blessed heart, may bring further satisfaction to her soul, and realize, at the appointed time, her dearest wish and fondest hopes for the Cause in your land. To complete the Temple, to clothe its naked dome, and terminate its exterior elaborate ornamentation, is the best and most effective way in which the American believers, the recipients of her untold favours, can demonstrate their fidelity to her memory and their gratitude for the inestimable blessings she showered upon them.

18. O WELL-LOVED friend,
The emotions that have possessed my grieving

heart are such that they cannot be put into words, and tongue and pen are helpless to describe them. The one consolation of this servant is the steadfastness and the redoubled services of those dearly-loved ones in Iran, and the good news of energetic efforts being exerted by the friends in that land. This is what dissipates the clouds of my grieving, and dispels the darkness of my anguish, and quiets the flames that consume my very being, and casts a ray of joy across the darkened sky of my agonized and stricken heart.

19. I WISH to add a few words in person as a token of my deepfelt appreciation of your loving message of sympathy in the great loss the family of 'Abdu'l-Bahá and myself have sustained. My prayer for each one of you is that the Almighty may aid you to perpetuate her glorious memory, to walk in her footsteps and to transmit to future generations the tradition she has bequeathed to us all.

20. I AM moved to add a few words with my own pen, to what has been written on my behalf, renewing my plea to you and through you, to each member of your beloved community, to prosecute, with undiminished vigour the enterprise which you have so splendidly inaugurated. The Greatest Holy Leaf, from her retreat of Glory, is watching over you, is interceding for every one of you, and is

expecting you to play your part in the great task, with which the prestige of her Father's glorious Cause is so closely associated. You have, while she lived amongst us, contributed to a remarkable degree to the brightening of her earthly life. By your persistent, your heroic endeavours you will, I am sure, bring added joy to her soul, and will vindicate afresh your undying loyalty to her memory.

21. THE passing of the beloved Khánum has plunged me in unspeakable sorrow. What a gap she has left behind her! It is terrible to contemplate. Your message, which I greatly value, lessened considerably the burden of my grief as I am fully conscious of the extent to which you have, in so many different ways, contributed to her physical well-being, and to the joy and satisfaction of her soul. We are all indebted to you for the many evidences of your loving and unfailing solicitude for her welfare, and we can only pray at her grave that her spirit may intercede for you before the throne of her glorious Father, and aid you to accomplish still greater things for a Cause, in the path of which she toiled and suffered all the days of her precious life.

22. I GREATLY value the expression of your loving sympathy and am greatly relieved by the sentiments your message conveyed. I will pray that you may be assisted, individually and collectively, to follow her inspiring example, to bring happiness

to her soul, and to proclaim far and wide the purity of her life, the immensity of her love, and the supreme nobility of her character.

23. I WISH to express to your distinguished assembly my gratitude for the action they have taken in reproducing in facsimile my humble tribute to the Greatest Holy Leaf. The hundred copies you sent me have been received and are splendid reproductions of the original. The finest and most enduring tribute which can be paid to her memory lies within the grasp, and constitutes the supreme opportunity, of the American believers. Her earthly life, as it drew to a close, was much brightened by the brilliant accomplishments of her devoted lovers in the American continent. May her pure angelic soul in the realms beyond derive added satisfaction from the uninterrupted progress and the eventual completion of an enterprise on which she had centred the one remaining joy of her life.

24. O YE who share my anguish and are my comforters in my distress and bereavement! In these past few months, from the day of the passing of that fairest fruit of the Undying Tree, of the setting of that wondrous Star in the heavens of endless glory, and of that bright Ray from the well spring of pre-existent light, ['Abdu'l-Bahá], the Ancient Beauty, the Most Great Name—may the spirits of

the Concourse on High be sacrificed for Him—has witnessed what has come upon me, whom she had surrounded at all times with her loving-kindness, her unceasing favours, and what a wound this loss has inflicted on my suffering heart. This parting from her has left my whole being in turmoil, burning with the fire of my love and longing for her. When, in the morning and the evening, I call her beloved face to mind, and let her smiles, that nourished the spirit, pass again before my eyes, and I think over all her bounty to me, all her unnumbered kindnesses, and remember that astonishing meekness she showed in her sufferings—then the flames of yearning love are kindled yet again, and sighs come out of my heart, and tears flow from my eyes, so that all control is lost and I sink into a sea of anguish without end.

Bearing witness to this, at this very moment, is her own pure and radiant soul, her bright and sacred spirit, that soars in the atmosphere of the invisible realm, and gazes, from beyond the throne of the Most High, upon me and upon those others on earth who are enamoured of her well-beloved name.

O thou Scion of Bahá! I weep over thee in the night season, as do the bereaved; and at break of day I cry out unto thee with the tongue of my heart, my limbs and members, and again and again I repeat thy well-loved name, and I groan over the loss of thee, over thy meekness and ordeals, and how thou didst love me, over the sufferings thou didst bear, and the terrible calamities, and the wretchedness and the griefs, and the abasement, and the rejection—and all this only and solely for the sake of thy Lord and because of thy burning love for those, out of all of creation, who shared in thine ardour.

Whensoever, in sleep, I call to mind and see thy smiling face, whensoever, by day or night, I circumambulate thine honoured tomb, then in the innermost depths of my being are rekindled the fires of yearning, and the cord of my patience is severed, and again the tears come and all the world grows dark before my eyes. And whensoever I remember what blows were rained upon thee at the close of thy days, the discomforts, trials and illnesses—and I picture thy surroundings now, in the Sanctuary on High, in the midmost heart of Heaven, beside the pavilions of grandeur and might; and I behold thy present glory, thy deliverance, the delights, the bounties, the bestowals, the majesty and dominion and power, the joy, thine exultation, and thy triumph—then the burden of my grieving is lightened, the cloud of sorrow is dispelled, the heat of my torment abates. Then is my tongue loosed to praise and thank thee, and thy Lord, Him Who did fashion thee and did prefer thee to all other handmaidens, and did give thee to drink from His sweet-scented lips, Who withdrew the veil of concealment from thy true being and made thee to be a true example for all thy kin to follow, and caused thee to be the fragrance of His garment for all of creation.

And at such times I strengthen my resolve to follow in thy footsteps, and to continue onward in the pathway of thy love; to take thee as my model, and to acquire the qualities, and to make manifest that which thou didst desire for the triumph of this exalted and exacting, this most resplendent, sacred, and wondrous Cause.

Then intercede thou for me before the throne of the Almighty, O thou who, within the Company on High, dost intercede for all of humankind. Deliver me from the throes of my mourning, and confer upon me and those who love thee in this nether world what will remove our afflictions, and bring assurance to our hearts, and quiet the winds of our sorrows, and console our eyes, and fulfil our hopes both in this world and the world to come—O thou whom God hast singled out from amongst all the countenances of the Abhá Paradise, and hast honoured in both His earth and His Kingdom on high, and of whom He has made mention in the Crimson Book, in words which wafted the scent of musk and scattered its fragrance over all the dwellers on earth!

O thou Greatest Holy Leaf! If I cry at every moment out of a hundred mouths, and from each of these mouths I speak with a hundred thousand tongues, yet I could never describe nor celebrate thy heavenly qualities, which are known to none save only the Lord God; nor could I befittingly tell of even the transient foam from out the ocean of thine endless favour and grace.

Except for a very few, whose habitation is in the highest retreats of holiness, and who circle, in the furthermost Sanctuary, by day and by night about the throne of God, and are fed at the hand of the

Abhá Beauty on purest milk—except for these, no soul of this nether world has known or recognized thine immaculate, thy most sacred essence, nor has any befittingly perceived that ambergris fragrance of thy noble qualities, which richly anoints thy brow, and which issues from the divine wellspring of mystic musk; nor has any caught its sweetness.

To this bear witness the Company on High, and beyond them God Himself, the Supreme Lord of all the heavens and the earths: that during all thy days, from thine earliest years until the close of thy life, thou didst personify the attributes of thy Father, the Matchless, the Mighty. Thou wert the fruit of His Tree, thou wert the lamp of His love, thou wert the symbol of His serenity, and of His meekness, the pathway of His guidance, the channel of His blessings, the sweet scent of His robe, the refuge of His loved ones and His handmaidens, the mantle of His generosity and grace.

O thou Remnant of the divine light, O thou fruit of the Cause of our All-Compelling Lord! From the hour when thy days did set, on the horizon of this Snow-White, this unique and Sacred Spot, our days have turned to night, our joys to great consternation; our eyes have grown blind with sorrow at thy passing, for it has brought back that supreme affliction yet again, that direst convulsion, the departing of thy compassionate Brother, our Merciful Master. And there is no refuge for us anywhere except for the breathings of thy spirit, the spotless, the excellently bright; no shelter for us anywhere, but through thine intercession, that God may inspire us with His own patience, and ordain for us in the other life the reward of meeting thee again, of attaining thy presence, of gazing on thy countenance, and partaking of thy light.

O thou Maid of Bahá! The best and choicest of praises, and the most excellent and most glorious of salutations, rest upon thee, O thou solace of mine eyes, and beloved of my soul! Thy grace to me was plenteous, it can never be concealed; thy love for me was great, it can never be forgotten. Blessed, a thousand times blessed, is he who loves thee, and partakes of thy splendours, and sings the praises of thy qualities, and extols thy worth, and follows in thy footsteps; who testifies to the wrongs thou didst suffer, and visits thy resting-place, and circles around thine exalted tomb, by day and by night. Woe unto him, retribution be his, who disputes thy rank and station, and denies thine excellence, and turns himself aside from thy clear, thy luminous and straight path.

O ye distracted lovers of that winsome countenance! It is meet and fitting that in the gatherings of the loved ones of God and the handmaids of the Merciful in all the countries and lands of the East, these shining words and clear tokens from the Supreme Pen and His Interpreter's wonder-working hand—verses which were revealed for that priceless treasure of the Kingdom—should be repeatedly recited, most movingly with devotion and lowliness, and great attention and care, so as to perpetuate her blessed memory, and extol her station, and out of love also for her incomparable beauty.

May the honoured members of the Central Assembly of Iran circulate these Writings, immediately and with great care, to the countries of the East, through their Local Spiritual Assemblies; for this task is a great bounty especially set apart for the trustees of His devoted loved ones in that noble homeland. May God reward them with excellent rewards, in both this world of His, and in His Kingdom.

25. MOVED by an unalterable devotion to the memory of the Greatest Holy Leaf, I feel prompted to share with you, and through you with the concourse of her steadfast lovers throughout the West, these significant passages[1] which I have gleaned from various Tablets revealed in her honour by Bahá'u'lláh and 'Abdu'l-Bahá.

Impregnated with that love after which the soul of a humanity in travail now hungers, these passages disclose, to the extent that our finite minds can comprehend, the nature of that mystic bond which, on one hand, united her with the Spirit of her almighty Father and, on the other, linked her so closely with her glorious Brother, the perfect Exemplar of that Spirit.

The memory of her who was a pattern of

[1] Included in Sections I and II.

goodness, of a pure and holy life, who was the embodiment of such heavenly virtues as only the privileged inmates of the uppermost chambers in the Abhá Paradise can fully appreciate, will long live enshrined in these immortal words—a memory the ennobling influence of which will remain an inspiration and a solace amid the wreckage of a sadly shaken world.

Conscious of the predominating share assumed, in recent years, by the American believers in alleviating the burden which that most exalted Leaf bore so heroically in the evening of her life, I can do no better than entrust into their hands these prized testimonies of the Founder of our Faith and of the Centre of His Covenant. I feel confident that their elected representatives will take whatever measures are required for their prompt and wide circulation among their brethren throughout the West. They will, thereby, be contributing still further to the repayment of the great debt they owe her in the prosecution of a mighty and divinely-appointed task.

26. IT was through the arrival of these pilgrims,[1] and these alone, that the gloom which had enveloped the disconsolate members of 'Abdu'l-Bahá's family was finally dispelled. Through the agency of these successive visitors the Greatest Holy Leaf, who alone with her Brother among the

[1] From the West, after the ascension of Bahá'u'lláh.

members of her Father's household had to confront the rebellion of almost the entire company of her relatives and associates, found that consolation which so powerfully sustained her till the very close of her life.

27. WITH 'Abdu'l-Bahá's ascension, and more particularly with the passing of His well-beloved and illustrious sister the Most Exalted Leaf—the last survivor of a glorious and heroic age—there draws to a close the first and most moving chapter of Bahá'í history, marking the conclusion of the Primitive, the Apostolic Age of the Faith of Bahá'u'lláh.

28. THE Fund associated with the beloved name of the Greatest Holy Leaf has been launched. The uninterrupted continuation to its very end of so laudable an enterprise is now assured. The poignant memories of one whose heart so greatly rejoiced at the rearing of the superstructure of this sacred House [the House of Worship in Wilmette, Illinois] will so energize the final exertions required to complete it as to dissipate any doubt that may yet linger in any mind as to the capacity of its builders to worthily consummate their task.

29. BLESSED REMAINS PUREST BRANCH AND MASTER'S MOTHER SAFELY TRANSFERRED HALLOWED

PRECINCTS SHRINES MOUNT CARMEL. LONG INFLICTED
HUMILIATION WIPED AWAY. MACHINATIONS COVE-
NANT-BREAKERS FRUSTRATE PLAN DEFEATED. CHER-
ISHED WISH GREATEST HOLY LEAF FULFILLED. SISTER
BROTHER MOTHER WIFE 'ABDU'L-BAHÁ REUNITED ONE
SPOT DESIGNED CONSTITUTE FOCAL CENTRE BAHÁ'Í
ADMINISTRATIVE INSTITUTIONS AT FAITH'S WORLD
CENTRE. SHARE JOYFUL NEWS ENTIRE BODY AMERICAN
BELIEVERS.

30. O LOVED ones of God, These two precious
and most exalted treasures,[1] these two keepsakes of
the sacred Beauty of Abhá, have now been joined
to the third trust from Him, that is, to the daughter
of Bahá and His remnant, the token of the Master's
Remembrance.

Their resting-places are in one area, on an
elevation close by the Spot round which do circle the
Concourse on High, and facing the Qiblih of the
people of Bahá—'Akká, the resplendent city, and
the sanctified, the luminous, the Most Holy Shrine.

Within the shadow of these honoured tombs has
also been laid the remains of the consort[2] of Him
round Whom all names revolve.

For joy, the Hill of God is stirred at so high an
honour, and for this most great bestowal the
mountain of the Lord is in rapture and ecstasy.

[1] The remains of the Purest Branch and those of Navváb.
[2] Munírih Khánum.

31. His[1] nine-year-old son, later surnamed the 'Most Great Branch', destined to become the Centre of His Covenant and authorized Interpreter of His teachings, together with His seven-year-old sister, known in later years by the same title[2] as that of her illustrious mother, and whose services until the ripe old age of four score years and six, no less than her exalted parentage, entitle her to the distinction of ranking as the outstanding heroine of the Bahá'í Dispensation, were ... included among the exiles who were now bidding their last farewell to their native country.

32. ... as a further testimony to the majestic unfoldment and progressive consolidation of the stupendous undertaking launched by Bahá'u'lláh on that holy mountain, may be mentioned the selection of a portion of the school property situated in the precincts of the Shrine of the Báb as a permanent resting-place for the Greatest Holy Leaf, the *'well-beloved'* sister of 'Abdu'l-Bahá, the *'Leaf that hath sprung'* from the *'Pre-existent Root'*, the *'fragrance'* of Bahá'u'lláh's *'shining robe'*, elevated by Him to a *'station such as none other woman hath surpassed'*, and comparable in rank to those immortal heroines such as Sarah, Ásíyih, the Virgin Mary, Fáṭimih and Ṭáhirih, each of whom has outshone every member of her sex in previous Dispensations.

[1] Bahá'u'lláh's.
[2] The Most Exalted Leaf.

33. THE raising of this Edifice[1] will in turn herald the construction, in the course of successive epochs of the Formative Age of the Faith, of several other structures . . .

These Edifices will, in the shape of a far-flung arc, and following a harmonizing style of architecture, surround the resting-places of the Greatest Holy Leaf, ranking as foremost among the members of her sex in the Bahá'í Dispensation, of her Brother, offered up as a ransom by Bahá'u'lláh for the quickening of the world and its unification, and of their Mother, proclaimed by Him to be His chosen 'consort in all the worlds of God'.

[1] The International Archives Building.

IV

Passages from letters
written on behalf of
SHOGHI EFFENDI

IV

Passages from letters
written on behalf of
SHOGHI EFFENDI

1. YOUR touching words in connection with the sudden removal of the Greatest Holy Leaf from their[1] midst have greatly alleviated the burden of sorrow that weighs so heavily upon their hearts and have demonstrated that in their great and irreparable loss the friends are faithfully sharing their sorrow and grief.

The passing of the Greatest Holy Leaf, so tragic in its suddenness, has, indeed, divested the Holy Family of its unique adornment and the Bahá'í world at large of one of its noblest and most precious members. She was to us all not only a true friend but the real embodiment of those traits and characteristics, of that genuine and profound love that was born of God, and that we had learned to admire in the Master . . .

In this great loss that the followers of the Faith both in East and West have come to suffer our Guardian's share is the greatest and perhaps the most cruel. His sole comfort, in this great calamity, is to

[1] Members of the Holy Family.

see the friends unitedly working for the spread of a Cause for which our departed Khánum had given up all her life, and for the triumph of which she cherished the highest hopes. The expressions of zealous enthusiasm and hope, of genuine self-abnegation and love that the American believers and especially our precious sister Mrs Agnes Parsons demonstrated in their last Convention meeting have greatly brightened the closing days of her life.[1] Shoghi Effendi trusts that her memory will increasingly serve to cheer and hearten the friends in their ever-widening activities.

2. THE passing of the Greatest Holy Leaf, so cruel in the feelings of unalterable grief that it has evoked, is, indeed, a tremendous loss to us all and particularly to our Guardian. Her presence among us was such a source of inspiration and joy that we cannot too deeply grieve the immensity of our loss. She was a real mother to every one of us, a comforter in our pains and anxieties, and a friend in our moments of utter loneliness and despair. But alas!

[1] Refers to the Annual Convention held in April 1932, at which the delegates and friends responded in an impressive manner to the need of the Fund associated with the name of the Greatest Holy Leaf, initiated in order to complete the exterior ornamentation of the House of Worship in Wilmette, Illinois. Mrs Parsons spontaneously removed a valuable pearl necklace from her neck to assist in meeting the Fund's goal. See *Bahá'í News*, No. 62, May 1932 for a report of that Convention.

We failed to appreciate adequately what her presence among us meant and it is only now, when she has gone for ever, that we come to realize the irreparable character of our loss.

And yet, however deep our consciousness of her unexpected removal from our midst may be, we cannot but feel certain that from her heavenly retreat she is continually showering her blessings upon everyone of us and is interceding on our behalf so that we may recover our energies and unanimously arise and dedicate our lives to the service of her Father's glorious Cause.

Her memory will, assuredly, continue to inspire us for many, many long years and will prove, when the hour of adversity is at its darkest, to be our best sustainer.

May her glorious spirit inspire us with faith and hope, steel our energies and enable us to make every sacrifice in the path lighted by her saintly and eventful life.

3. THE ascension of the Greatest Holy Leaf is, indeed, an irreparable loss to us all and will continue to be deeply felt for many, many long years. Her presence among us was such a source of blessings and inspiration! She was to every one of us not only a friend but a real mother, through whose maternal care and love we had learned to feel and experience that consuming love which is born of God and which alone can galvanize the souls of men.

Her departure from our midst, though cruel and heart-rending in its immediate results cannot but ultimately serve the very best interests of the Cause. For this invincible Faith of God has, ever since its inception in darkest Persia, grown and flourished amidst all sorts of tribulations and sufferings and has welcomed all these as providential forces destined to ensure its unity, promote its interests and consolidate its work.

Let us, therefore, not remain disconsolate and hopeless and withstand in a heroic way the shock occasioned by the passing of our beloved Khánum. Her ascension is a challenge to us all, a challenge to our faith, to our sincerity and to our love.

May her memory continue to strengthen and deepen our spiritual insight and enable us to render the Faith as many services as we can.

4. His grief is too immense and his loss too heavy to be adequately expressed in words. But the many letters of condolence he has already received, and especially your message that indicated your profound attachment to our departed Khánum, greatly comforted his sorrow-stricken heart and gave him the assurance that in this calamitous event the friends are amply sharing his grief.

However irreparable and heart-rending our loss may be, we cannot but thank God for having released our beloved Holy Leaf from the oppression and bondage of this world. For more than eighty years this Exalted Leaf bore with a fortitude that bewildered every one who had the privilege of knowing her, sufferings and tribulations that few of our present-day believers did experience. And yet, what a joy and what a saintlike attitude she manifested all through her life. Her angelic face was so calm, so serene in the very midst of sufferings and pains. Not that she lacked tenderness of heart and sympathy. But she could overcome her feelings and this because she had put all her trust in God.

And now that she has gone for ever we should rejoice at the thought that she is still living in our hearts and is animating our soul with a devotion, a courage, and a hope of which we are in such a dire need in these days of sufferings and hardships.

May the memory of her saintly life inspire you with faith and hope, cheer and strengthen your heart and make of you a servant worthy to promote and consolidate the interests of the Faith!

5. THE irreparable loss which the Faith has suffered through the passing of the Greatest Holy Leaf is too immense to be adequately expressed in words, and we cannot fully realize its significance at the present stage of the evolution of the Cause. Future generations stand in a better position to appreciate what her significance was during the early days of the Revelation and especially after the ascension of 'Abdu'l-Bahá.

And now that she has gone for ever and is in direct communion with God we should rejoice at the thought that from the Realm Above she is watching over us all and is sending us her blessings.

May the memory of her saintly life be our comforter in our hours of sadness and despair, and may we learn through her example how to live the true life of the spirit, of self-abnegation and of service.

6.   IN these days, when we are all mourning the loss of our beloved Greatest Holy Leaf, Shoghi Effendi's sole comfort is to see the friends as ever devoted and active and striving day and night to promote the teachings of the Cause.

However cruel our separation from Bahíyyih K͟hánum may be, especially at a time when her presence among us was such a source of inspiration and strength, yet we feel confident that from her Heavenly Retreat she is sending us her blessings and is quickening our weary souls.

Concerning the suspension of festivities for a period of nine months it should be made clear that what is meant by this is that all gatherings, whether outdoor or indoor, which are not of a strictly devotional character should be abolished all through the period of our mourning. However, meetings and services that are wholly spiritual as well as those that are necessary for the carrying on of the administration should continue to be held as usual.

7. YOUR message of condolence and sympathy, dated July 22nd, 1932 which so fully conveyed your profound grief at the loss occasioned by the unexpected passing of the Greatest Holy Leaf was received and read with great interest. The Guardian's sorrow was much relieved and the burden of his agonizing pain immensely alleviated. He sincerely hopes that out of the pangs of this crushing calamity the Faith will strengthen its foundations and extend the sphere of its ever-widening influence.

Our loss is, indeed, immense and even irreparable. But our joy should also be great, for the Greatest Holy Leaf has at least been released from the bondage of this world after more than eighty years of continued suffering. It would take me too long to relate in their fullness those incidents which eloquently proclaim her as one of the greatest sufferers the world has yet seen. And yet, with what a fortitude she bore all these tribulations for she was confident in the grace of God.

Though now gone for ever from our midst we should be hopeful that from her Celestial Realm she will send us her blessings and will extend to us her help. Her memory will continue to cheer and strengthen our souls, deepen our spiritual insight and bring us to a strong determination to serve till the very last breath of our life a Cause for which our departed Khánum gave up her entire existence and for the future of which she cherished the brightest hopes.

8. ... THE news of the Memorial Service you had held for the Greatest Holy Leaf gave him the assurance that the friends are faithfully sharing his grief and are demonstrating in a befitting manner their profound devotion to one whose very life was an example of faithfulness and sincerity, of self-abnegation and love.

The ascension of the Greatest Holy Leaf is, indeed, both a calamity and a blessing. It is an overwhelming calamity since it has deprived us of the presence in our very midst of the last Remnant of that Heroic age of the Cause that gave birth to so many noble and faithful souls. The mere presence of our beloved Khánum among us was a source of inspiration and blessing. And now that she has gone we cannot too deeply deplore the immensity of our loss.

But thanks to God for having released her, after so many long years of agonizing pain, of the bondage of this world and given her the priceless privilege of being in direct communion with God.

May her everlasting spirit continue to guide our efforts and enable us to serve a Cause, for which she suffered so much, with all our might, our enthusiasm and hope.

9. THE letter from that spiritual friend has reached the beloved Guardian, and he is aware of your bitter grieving over the calamitous news that a most glorious fruit of the Holy Tree, the Most Exalted Leaf, the Remnant of Bahá, has passed away.

This disastrous event has had an effect on the Guardian so terrible that no pen can describe it nor paper bear the words; for that bright and surpassingly fair presence, that quintessence of the perfections and attributes of God, was his close companion, and the consolation of his heart, so that his separation from her whom the world wronged, and the ascension of that loved one of the community of love, was unspeakably hard for him to bear.

She was a divine trust, a treasure of the Kingdom, and she spent all the days of her precious life as an exile and a captive, and her every priceless hour was passed under tests and afflictions and ordeals that she endured at the hands of merciless foes. From early childhood she had her share of the sufferings of Bahá'u'lláh, subjected even as He was to hardships and calamities, and she was as well the partner in sorrows and tribulations of 'Abdu'l-Bahá.

For her there was never a night of peaceful sleep, for her no day when she found rest, and always, like a moth, would her comely person circle about the bright candle of the Faith. The words of her mouth were ever to glorify the Abhá Beauty, her only thought and her high purpose were to proclaim the Cause of God and to protect His Law, while the dearest wish of her glowing heart was to waft far and wide the sweet breathings of the Lord.

Her heavenly ways were a model for the people of Bahá, and those who dwell in the pavilions of devotion and the denizens of the Abhá Paradise found in her celestial attributes their prototype and their guide. Glory be to God, Who created her, fashioned her, called her into being, sent her forth and revealed her, whose like the eye of the world had never seen.

The Guardian sends his message of consolation to your honoured self and all the friends, and he says that it is fitting that the righteous should hold fast to the cord of resignation and acquiescence, and adorn themselves with the ornaments of faithfulness and servitude, and take for their example that priceless treasure of the Kingdom.

10. THE letter dated 5 August 1932, from that spiritual friend has been received by the Guardian of the Cause of God, may our lives be sacrificed for him, and he has been informed of your receiving his telegram regarding the ascension of that matchless fruit of the Tree of Glory, the Most Exalted Leaf.

There is no question but that the burden of grief on his sorrowing heart, because of this terrible ordeal, this great calamity, is heavier than minds can conceive, or words can tell. That gem of immortality, that precious and exalted being, was the one consolation, the one companion of the Guardian in his sorrow-filled life; and she, with her sweet encouragement, her gentle words, her never-ceasing, soothing care of him, her smiles that came like fair winds from heavenly gardens, could always gladden and refresh his spirit.

No one has understood the tender, spiritual and celestial bond between the Guardian and her who was the Remnant of Bahá, nor can any mind conceive that plane of being, nor reckon its sublimity.

During her whole life span, that heavenly being was subjected to ordeals and tribulations. She confronted the attacks of the hostile, and she suffered afflictions any one of which could well have shattered a mountain of iron. And yet the sweet and comely face of that spirit-like dove of holiness, was wreathed till her very last hour in life-giving smiles, nor did that patience and endurance, that greatness, that majesty and dignity, ever desert her delicate and fragile person.

She who was the trust left by Bahá'u'lláh had no other aim nor goal but these: to proclaim the Cause of God and exalt His Word; to praise and glorify the Blessed Beauty's name; to bear 'Abdu'l-Bahá in mind and serve Him ever; to pity the sorely-troubled and give them endless, loving care; to cherish and comfort them, and bring them joy. There is, then, good reason, that with the passing of this peerless gem, this precious, matchless pearl, we should rend our garments in mourning, and that our eyes should stream with bitter tears.

The Guardian conveys his message of condolence, and says that in this severest of afflictions, it would befit the people of Bahá to hold fast to resignation and acquiescence, and to rise up and loyally serve the Faith, taking for their example that priceless treasure of the Abhá Paradise.

11. WHAT you had written concerning the memorial gatherings of men and women believers to mourn the Most Exalted Leaf, who was the peerless fruit of the Holy Tree, and to commemorate the ascension of her who was the most glorious trust left on earth by the Lord—may the souls of holy men and women be a sacrifice for her sacred resting-place—has been received by the Guardian.

It cannot be imagined to what a degree this terrible and calamitous event has saddened him, and, more than words can tell, clouded the radiance of his heart. For that holy being, that resplendent person, with all her heart and soul and endless love, had ever fostered and cherished him in the warm embrace of her celestial tenderness. She was his single, dear companion, she was his one and only consolation in the world, and that is why he is so burdened down with the passing of her high and stately presence, and why the departure of that comely spirit is so hard for him to bear.

She who was left in trust by Bahá'u'lláh was the symbol of His infinite compassion, the day star in the heaven of His bounty and grace. That sanctified spirit revealed the loving-kindness of Him who was the Beauty of the All-Glorious, and was the welling spring of the favours and bestowals of Him Who was the Lord, the Most High. She was the comforter of anyone who grieved, the solace of any with a broken heart. She, that Remnant of Bahá, was a loving mother to the orphan, and for the hapless and bewildered it was she who would find a way. Her holy life lit up the world; her heavenly qualities and ways were a standard for people all over the earth. Like a cloud of grace, she showered down gifts, and her bestowals, like the morning winds, refreshed the soul.

Stranger and friend alike were captured by her loving-kindness, her spiritual nature, her unceasing care for them and tender ways; enamoured of her great indulgence toward them, and how she favoured them and cherished them. The mind could only marvel at that subtle and ethereal being, at the majesty and greatness of her, and the heavenly modesty, and the forbearance and long suffering. Even in the thick of the worst ordeals, she would smile like an opening rose, and no matter how dark and calamitous the times, like a bright candle she would shed her light.

The Guardian sends messages of heartfelt condolence to all of you, and asks you to be submissive and acquiescent and patient, and loyally to arise and serve, and take for your model that precious treasure of the Abhá Paradise.

You had asked the Guardian as to the nine months of mourning, during which all Bahá'í festivities are

to be suspended. His answer is that this refers to nine
solar months. He says further that the blessed and
exalted Leaf ascended at one hour after midnight, on
the eve of Friday, July 15.

12. ... HE is eagerly awaiting to see the friends
as ever burning with the desire to serve a Cause for
the sake of which our departed Holy Leaf gave up
her entire existence.

May her glorious spirit cheer your hearts, strengthen your faith and inspire you with renewed
courage and hope.

13. HIS loss is too immense to be adequately
expressed in words. But his joy is also great. For
such calamitous events, though cruel in their
immediate effects, nevertheless, serve to stimulate
the friends and quicken their souls.

Ours, therefore, is the opportunity to arise and
serve the Cause and put all our trust in God. Surely,
He will guide our steps and will inspire us with the
necessary enthusiasm and strength.

May the immortal spirit of our departed
Khánum quicken our energies and give fresh lustre
to our endeavours for the greater extension of the
Cause.

14. THE profound sorrow occasioned by the sudden passing of the Greatest Holy Leaf, as well as the unnumbered messages of sympathy received from friends and believers in East and West, all of which the Guardian acknowledged in person, have caused the unavoidable delay in giving his immediate attention to various matters referred to in your communications to him. He deeply regrets the obstacles which stood in his way and which by their very nature he found them impossible to surmount.

15. THE Guardian of the Cause of God has received your letter of 21 July 1932, telling of your and the other friends' profound distress on receiving word of this calamity, this dire ordeal, that is, the ascension of the Most Exalted Leaf, that brightest fruit of the Eternal Tree.

It is certain that this anguish, this harrowing event, has reached into the very depths of his being, and oppressed and darkened his radiant heart more than words can ever tell. For the subtle and spiritual attachment that the Guardian felt for her, and the heavenly tenderness and affection between that lovely fruit of the divine Lote-Tree and himself, was a bond so strong as to defy description, nor can the mind encompass that exalted state. That secret is a secret well-concealed, a treasured mystery unplumbed, and to a plane such as this, the minds of the believers can never find their way. On this account the Guardian's anguish at being parted from that bright and comely denizen of Heaven is beyond our conceiving.

She who was a sparkling light of God, she who was so full of grace—that widespread ray of Heaven's splendour, that sign of God's mercy—was made to appear with all perfections, all goodly attributes, all blessed ways; and never had the world's eye gazed upon such a welling spring of tender love, of pity and compassion, and never will it behold again such a gem of loving-kindness, such a fount of God's munificence.

How many a night did she whom the world wronged spend as a prisoner, worn with care, tormented, banished from her home. How many a day did she live through as an exile and a captive! There was no venom of affliction, at the hands of this Faith's foes, that was not given her to drink, no arrow of cruelty but struck her holy breast. Yet in spite of the endless tribulations and disasters, she who was a spirit of holiness and a songster of Heaven, would even in the midst of dire ordeals, her face aglow, bloom like a rose.

The Guardian sends messages of consolation to you and all the friends in this bereavement, and he says that in this calamitous time all must bow down their heads and be acquiescent, arise in faithful service to His Cause, and model themselves upon that most exalted, sacred and resplendent presence.

16. THE Guardian's anguish, because of this tragic occurrence, is such that it can neither be plumbed nor described in words. That sublime and gloried Leaf, that precious jewel of the Kingdom, was the one great solace of his life; she was his glorious companion, and her disappearance, and the separation from her, and her ascending into the heavenly presence and court of her Lord was the direst ordeal to be visited upon the people of Bahá. Alas for any future time that might produce such a calamity, when the world's eye might see its like.

That sacred treasure, that jewel of Heaven, was the very sign and token of spiritual attributes and qualities and perfections, the very model of high honour and nobility and heavenly ways. The sufferings she bore in the pathway of God were the cruellest ones, the afflictions that assailed her were the severest of all. Fortitude was the rich dress she wore, serenity and tranquil strength were her splendid robe, virtue and detachment, purity and chastity, were all her jewels, and tenderness, care and love for humankind, her beauty's bright adornings.

The Guardian conveys his message of consolation and comfort, enjoining submission and acquiescence in this calamity, and the need for arising to serve and to be steadfast, and to take for our model that gem of the Abhá Paradise.

17. INDEED, the Greatest Holy Leaf, the Trust of Bahá'u'lláh amongst us, was the emblem of His boundless grace, a luminary shining in the heaven of

tender mercy and gracious providence, the embodiment of the manifold favours of the Abhá Beauty, a
repository of the bounty and loving-kindness so
characteristic of the Báb, the Exalted One. To
every disconsolate one she was an affectionate
comforter, to every heart-broken and grief-stricken
soul, a token of unfailing sympathy, of kindliness,
of cheer and comfort. Her blessed life was a source
of spiritual illumination for the whole world and her
noble traits and heavenly attributes served as a
shining example, an object of emulation for all
mankind. Like the showers of heavenly grace, her
generosity knew no bounds, and as the breeze of
celestial blessing and favour, she breathed a new life
into every soul. Both friends and strangers were
drawn by her sense of spirituality, her tenderness
and refinement, her unfailing solicitude, and were
attracted by the magic of her unbounded affection
and goodwill. That heavenly being displayed
throughout her life such evidence of glory and
dignity, such manifestations of majesty and greatness, such a degree of patience and resignation as
bewildered the minds and souls. In the midst of trials
her radiant face bore the likeness of a sweet rose and
in moments of sore tribulation she was resplendent
as a brilliant candle.

18. THE Guardian trusts that the explanation he
has given by wire regarding the suspension for a
period of nine months of Bahá'í religious festivity

has been made clear. The Nineteen Day Feast being of a quasi-administrative character should continue to be held, but should be conducted with the utmost simplicity and should be devoid of any features associated with feasts and entertainment. The celebration of Naw-Rúz, the anniversary of the birth of Bahá'u'lláh and of the Báb should be altogether cancelled as a token of our deep mourning for so distinguished and precious a member of Bahá'u'lláh's family. The period of nine months should be reckoned from the 15th of July to the 15th of April.

19. THE loss of the Greatest Holy Leaf will be bitterly felt by all those friends who had the pleasure and privilege to meet her. She always kept such a wonderful atmosphere of joy and hope around her that was bound to influence those that were present and help them to go out into the world with added zeal and determination to consecrate all in the path of God.

The only consolation of Shoghi Effendi is in the knowledge that she has been delivered from earthly worries and physical weakness and that she is now in the presence of Bahá'u'lláh, her Father and Lord, enjoying the infinite blessings of His eternal Kingdom.

20. EVEN though during these last years she was weak and most of the time confined to her room, yet

she was a source of constant joy and inspiration to those that met her. The Guardian feels her loss tremendously because the greatest part of his leisure hours he used to spend in her company.

His only comfort is that she has been delivered from the worries and weaknesses of a body that could no more withhold her spirit and help her to express all her desire in meeting the friends and serving them.

At present, in the presence of her Father and Lord we trust she is remembering us and asking for us His divine grace and blessings.

21.   THE passing away of the Greatest Holy Leaf was a loss every Bahá'í will feel deeply if only he stops to think about it. She was such a precious soul and so radiantly happy and hopeful even under most adverse circumstances. Every believer that came in contact with her left her presence with a more determined spirit of service and self-sacrifice. Both Shoghi Effendi and the rest of the Bahá'ís will mourn her loss bitterly. Their only consolation can be her own deliverance from a life of hardship and difficulties, and her entrance into a realm which is naught but eternal bliss and infinite divine grace.

22.   EVEN though the Greatest Holy Leaf has left us in body she is with us in spirit, inspiring us in our work and beseeching for us God's loving mercy and

fatherly care. She will never forget her loving friends nor leave them in their woes.

Shoghi Effendi was very sad to hear of your difficulties, especially as they have encompassed you at an age when you cannot confront them but must have comfort and peace. You should, however, take courage and resign to the will of God when you see what the Greatest Holy Leaf had to face during her life. All you may suffer is nothing compared to what she had to endure; and yet how joyous and hopeful she used always to be!

This is the way of the world. The greatest among us seems to be the one who has suffered most and withstood best the battles of life.

23. SHOGHI Effendi wishes me to acknowledge the receipt of your letter dated August 25th 1932 and to extend his deep appreciation for your kind words of sympathy. This loss is a thing that will be bitterly felt by every Bahá'í throughout the world, because she used to be a source of inspiration to every one of them. The mere coming into her presence and thinking of the trials and difficulties she had to pass through in her life, was sufficient to create in us new hope and arouse us to stronger determination to promote the Cause she suffered for.

24. YOU should be very happy to have had the privilege of meeting her upon this physical plane of

existence, for the world has seen only very few such souls who have suffered so much for the sake of God and yet kept their cheer and uttered words of hope and encouragement to those who were around them. What a source of inspiration she was to the pilgrims who came from the four corners of the world to seek spirituality and attain a new birth by visiting the Holy Shrines. They should surely remember those blessed moments they spent in her room or in her presence elsewhere, and remembering her suffering, take courage in confronting the problems of their life. May God help us all to follow her example and like her be a blessing to others.

25.   SURELY there is nothing that will console the Guardian more than the happy news that the Cause for which the Greatest Holy Leaf lived and suffered is gradually spreading and embracing the whole of the people of the world.

She is undoubtedly conscious of our activities, following our work and impatiently awaiting the result of our battles. Let her passing, therefore, be a source of added sacrifice and more energetic striving on the part of her devoted friends and lovers.

26.   THESE nine months during which the Guardian has asked the friends to discard feast days, are meant to be months of mourning for the passing away of the Greatest Holy Leaf. The friends should

also use it as a period of redoubled energy in serving the Cause in expression of our deep love for her as well as for the Cause she so much suffered for.

27. SURELY no matter what we say about her still we have not done justice to the abounding love she had and the services she rendered to Bahá'u'lláh and the Master. Her life was full of events, full of sacrifices in the path of God. Ever since her childhood she had to endure hardships and share the exile and persecution that Bahá'u'lláh had to suffer. In her face one could easily read the history of the Cause from its earliest days to the present moment.

Notwithstanding all this she never grumbled nor lost her faith in the future. She kept cheerful and tried to give cheer to others. She was a real source of inspiration to every person that met her.

The only adequate way to show our love and devotion to her is to arise and serve the Cause for which she so earnestly laboured during all her mortal life. Her deeds and sacrifices should act as examples for us to follow.

28. INDEED it would have been for you such a joy to meet the Greatest Holy Leaf during her earthly life, but the Guardian does not wish you to feel depressed about it; this beloved soul will from the Heaven of her Almighty Father guide you to serve the Cause which has been so dear to her. Shoghi

Effendi values your sincere sympathy in this irreparable loss; he hopes that we all will follow the example of her saintly life.

29. HE fully appreciates the deep sorrow that you, as well as the other friends, feel for the passing away of the Greatest Holy Leaf. All those who met her cannot feel but an emptiness in their hearts. She was always such a source of courage and hope to those pilgrims that came from all parts of the world and had the pleasure of meeting her, that they left her presence with added hope and greater determination to serve the Cause and sacrifice their all in its path. This was especially true of them after the passing away of the Master when they felt that she was the only worthy remnant of Bahá'u'lláh's immediate kin.

May her passing stir the friends to greater measures of sacrifice and direct their attention towards the spiritual duties that have been laid upon their shoulders.

30. HE is sure that all the Bahá'ís throughout the world share with him in this sorrow, for she was a source of comfort and inspiration to them all. No one left her presence without being deeply impressed by her spirit. All the sufferings that she had endured during her life and that had left their traces upon her feeble form, had not in the least affected her spirit of joy and hopefulness. She liked to see the people happy, and exerted all her efforts to make it easy for them to realize it.

How badly we need such souls in the world at present when it seems so full of sorrows and discouragements! Every one is suffering and no person to give them courage and brighten their hearts.

Shoghi Effendi hopes that the friends will follow her example and become a source of inspiration to the world at large, giving hope to the depressed and joy to the disconsolate. Moreover, he trusts that her passing will operate as a great impetus in our services to the Cause for which she suffered so long and so hard.

31. HE deeply appreciates your sincere, well-expressed reference, to the tribute he has written to the dearly beloved Greatest Holy Leaf. You cannot imagine to what an extent our dear Guardian has, in this loss, been deprived for ever of the sustaining influence and kindness that this Most Exalted Leaf used to shower daily upon him. In this beautiful Tribute we can trace the life of this beautiful soul, witness with anguish all the sufferings and deprivations that she has endured. Now we should, all of us, try in turn to follow her saintly path and direct all our energy to serve the Cause, which has been so dear to her.

32. ... HE was deeply touched by the strong attachment of the friends to one who, besides being

the beloved daughter of Bahá'u'lláh, exemplified perhaps more than anyone the true spirit that animates His teachings. His sincere hope is that your love for our departed Greatest Holy Leaf will attain such depth and intensity as to enable you to follow on her footsteps and to carry out with increasing devotion and vigour all that she cherished so much during the entire course of her earthly life. The memory of her saintly life will undoubtedly sustain and feed your energies and will provide you with that spiritual potency of which we are all in such a great need.

33. THE steps of her holy resting-place represent Local Spiritual Assemblies, not individual believers. The columns, that is the pillars, are like the National Spiritual Assemblies, while the dome, which is raised following the placing of the columns, symbolizes the Universal House of Justice which, in accordance with the Master's Will and Testament must be elected by the secondary Houses of Justice, that is, the National Spiritual Assemblies of East and West.

Monument marking the resting place of the Greatest Holy Leaf, erected on Mount Carmel by Shoghi Effendi, who said that its three stages symbolized the three-fold structure of Bahá'u'lláh's Administrative Order.

Views of the monument; above, floodlit at night; below, an
early photograph.

View of the monument looking northwards across the Bay of Haifa, to 'Akká.

Photograph of Bahá'u'lláh's Tablet, in His Own handwriting, to Bahíyyih Khánum, the text of which is carved and gilded around the pediment of her monument.

(see Dedication)

V

Letters of
THE GREATEST HOLY LEAF

V

Letters of
THE GREATEST HOLY LEAF

1. O LEAF of Paradise!

Loose your tongue at all times in gratitude for the blessings of the Beloved of the Worlds, for you are always mentioned in His Glorious and Sanctified Presence, and you are ever in the hearts of His maidservants. The pen is unable to describe the depths of our longing, nor can the tongue recount the love concealed within our hearts. Should you look into the mirror of your own heart, which is free from the defilements of this world of dust, you would clearly see the truth of what has been set forth.

From the time of your departure no day passes without mention being made of your name. Please God you may in your days and nights hold fast to the sure handle of detachment, and be occupied in the remembrance of God, the Wondrous, the All-Glorious.

There is no blessing greater than attainment unto His Holy Presence. Thank God you attained this bounty.

May the spiritually-minded son, Mírzá Badí'u'lláh, God willing, be always safe in the stronghold of God's care and protection.

2. I FEEL prompted to offer my sincere best wishes to you and to express the agony of separation that has deeply affected me. First of all let me say that I received with the hand of gratitude and thankfulness your kind letter which bore the full abundance of your love and amply portrayed the noble traits of your nature, so richly adorned with laudable characteristics. In truth, I always pay tribute to your excellent qualities and eagerly yearn to set my eyes upon your countenance. I often recall those days when I had the delightful pleasure of your company and indulged in the fruits of your brilliant sense of humour. Perhaps the days of reunion shall come again through the favour of the Lord of grace and bounty. I fervently pray that God—glorified and exalted be He—may endue your life with vigour and happiness and enable you to achieve your heart's desire. Moreover, I beseech Him—exalted is He—to grant me the pleasure of meeting you again very soon. Indeed, He is nigh and readily answers the call. I hereby offer my best greetings and befitting salutations to your revered person, and may God perpetuate your life. Every one here enquires about your distinguished self and sends high expressions of praise and compliment to you. May God prolong your life.

3. THE letter in which that leaf had expressed the ardent longing of her heart and revealed the depth of her devotion has received my eager attention.

Indeed, the voice of lamentation that the loved ones of God and His devoted servants have raised on the occasion of this terrible adversity, this grievous calamity, has caused the fire of His bereavement to rage more fiercely than ever. In reality no pen can depict the poignant feeling that surges in our hearts. Every expression would prove utterly inadequate, even less than the eye of a needle, inasmuch as words and syllables are incapable of conveying the intensity of this dire suffering. They are but a tiny drop compared to an ocean. Even in the vast immensity of inner significances and expositions nothing can portray this calamitous event. Moreover, the tale of how these prisoners have been consumed by the fire of bereavement is interminable. During this dark and dreadful calamity, and to this God bears me witness, our souls melted and our eyes unceasingly rained with tears.

Nevertheless, when faced with the irrevocable decree of the Almighty, the vesture that best befits us in this world is the vesture of patience and submission, and the most meritorious of all deeds is to commit our affairs into His hands and to surrender ourselves to His Will. Therefore, it behoves that leaf to take fast hold on the handle of resignation and radiant acquiescence and to strictly adhere to the cord of patience and long-suffering. God willing, through His aid and heavenly confirmation you may be enabled to exalt His Word and to render exemplary service to His Cause, that perchance the ears of all created things may be purged of the tales of bygone ages and become endued with the capacity to hearken to the holy verses that the Lord of all men has proclaimed. Indeed, this is the underlying purpose of man's existence during the brief period of his earthly life. Please God, we may all be confirmed and aided to achieve this.

Every manner of description that I use, and every form of symbolic expression that I conceive will fail to convey the extent of the ardent love and affection that I cherish for you; however, it causes the fire of love to glow more intensely and to burn more brightly. Therefore, I had better confine myself to these few lines.

At the court of the presence of the Most Mighty Branch—may the lives of them that yearn after Him and are wholly devoted to Him be sacrificed for His holy presence—your name has been mentioned and you became the recipient of His special favours.

4. DESPITE our overwhelming sorrows and afflictions, our heart-burning and depth of woes, you are always in our thoughts and we call to mind your cheerful face. When we visit the Most Holy Shrine, the Point round which revolve the people of the world, we offer our prayers, and visit that Sacred Spot on your behalf, and on behalf of all the friends, particularly the well-assured, the faithful and loyal

handmaids of the Merciful. We have prayed and will continue to pray at the Threshold of the Tomb of the Blessed Beauty for your success, and that of your relatives. Likewise in the presence of 'Him Whom God hath purposed' you are always remembered. Several days ago He retired to the Cave of Khiḍr,[1] and that verdant spot has been blessed by the steps of our Master, 'Him round Whom all names revolve'. He intends to stay there for a while, so that He may have some respite from His countless concerns and cares.

For the most part your previous letters have been answered, but you have not acknowledged receipt. This letter is in reply to your recent missive, so that you will be confident that we are, under all conditions, thinking of you.

Should you enquire about these bereaved ones, through the grace of the Lord and the bounties of His divine Mystery, we are all well, but our grief knows no bounds. We supplicate at the Threshold of the Eternal and Almighty Beloved that He may unlock before us the doors of delight, awaken the heedless and those in deep slumber, and grant the exponents of violation a sense of justice, so that its dust may settle down, that this dissension be wiped out, and once again we may taste the sweetness of the days of bliss.

O Lord! Graciously enable this servant of Thine as well as those who supplicate tearfully before Thy face and have turned towards Thee in their affliction

[1] Elijah.

to achieve unity, harmony, friendliness and fellowship, that they may magnify Thy virtues in the
daytime and in the night season, may chant Thy holy
words, may recite verses from Thy heavenly Book,
may eagerly set their hearts toward the retreats of
Thy holiness, yearning to behold the vision of Thy
grandeur. O Lord! Fulfil their hearts' desires, gladden
their bosoms with the shining splendour of the
Centre of Thy Covenant, illumine their eyes and
rejoice their souls with the goodly gifts of the light of
harmony. Verily Thou art the Lord of the Day of
Judgement.

5.   It is my earnest hope that you, His distinguished leaf, together with the other maidservants of
the All-Merciful in that land, may be so enkindled by
the flame set ablaze by the hand of God as to illumine
the whole world through the quickening energy of
the love of God, and that through the eloquence of
your speech, the fluency of your tongue, and the
confirmations of the Holy Spirit you will be empow-
ered to expound divine wisdom in such manner
that men of eloquence, and the scholars and sages of
the world, will be lost in bewilderment. This indeed
would not be hard for Him.

6.   O EXALTED leaf, O distinguished friend! May
the glory of God and His praise, His bounty and

blessing rest upon you inasmuch as you have remained faithful to the Covenant of God and His Testament.

Your letter so fine and ornate, a gift from the Paradise of the love of God, and a dear token of the celestial Garden of divine knowledge, has been received, and perfumed with its spiritual and ethereal fragrance the nostrils of this maidservant of God, this yearning prisoner.

Praise be to God that He has enabled you, His well-assured leaf, to magnify at all times the glory of His gracious countenance, has sustained your life through the remembrance of His Beauty, has suffered you to rid yourself of all attachment to any one save Him that you may continually commune with His love. He has graciously assisted you to remain faithful to His weighty and irrefutable Testament, to cling tenaciously to the hem of the robe of the Centre of the Covenant of God, the All-Bountiful, and to fix your gaze entirely upon the luminous face of 'Him Whom God hath purposed', the One 'Who hath branched from the pre-existent Root'. In truth, a myriad praises and thanksgiving should be offered in appreciation of this outpouring of divine favours and blessings. We implore the Kingdom of our Lord, the All-Glorious, that He may continually waft upon you His vitalizing breaths, may enrapture you by the uplifting transports of His delight, may quicken you through His Holy Spirit and may grant you confirmation to serve His maidservants and His leaves.

7.   MAY my life be sacrificed for those leaves who are steadfast in the Covenant of God—they whom the slander of the slanderer hinders not from holding fast to His divine Testament.

I yield praise to God and offer thanksgiving to the Abhá Beloved—may my spirit be offered up for every atom of the dust of His holy Threshold —inasmuch as the animating breeze of holiness has wafted from the rose-garden of your love and fellowship. By this is meant that your letter—a letter fraught with expressions of loving-kindness that that loved one of my heart and soul penned with such tender affection—has been received. It brought immense happiness to the grief-stricken heart of this yearning prisoner and by perusing its contents my whole being has been flooded with ineffable glad-ness. Indeed, the nostrils of my heart have been perfumed by its sweet savours and the channel of my soul has become redolent with its vitalizing per-fume, inasmuch as from its inner meaning the fragrances of heavenly praise and adoration were inhaled and from its words the sweet smell of attraction to the love of God was perceived. In truth, every letter which serves to magnify the glory of the Ancient Beauty or to extol the virtues of the Most Great Name is sweeter than honey, for it imparts sweetness to the palate of the soul.

In brief, we all rejoice to know that you and the other handmaids of God in that region are enjoying good health, that they are all firm and steadfast in the Cause of God, are shining brightly and are enraptured by His love; for this token of grace we have offered boundless praise at the Threshold of our forgiving Lord. We are well acquainted with the matters you have mentioned in your letter, and in the luminous and holy presence of the peerless Servant of His Threshold, our Master, 'Abdu'l-Bahá—may my life be sacrificed for Him—your name and the names of all the handmaids of God and of His enraptured leaves have been mentioned and words of praise were expressed by Him in your favour. Be well assured that you are always remembered at the spiritual meetings and gatherings of the friends.

8.   FROM this hallowed and snow-white Spot, this blessed, heavenly Garden, wherefrom the fragrance of God is diffused to all regions, I hail you with salutations, most tender, most wondrous, and most glorious, and impart to you the most joyful tiding. This tiding serves as the sweet-smelling savour of His raiment to them that long to behold His face, it represents the highest aspiration of His steadfast leaves, it is the animating impulse for the happiness of the world, it is the source of ineffable gladness to the people of Bahá, a remedy to the afflicted, and a refreshing draught for the thirsty. By the righteousness of God, O beloved friend, through this glad-tiding the ailing are cured and every mouldering bone is quickened. This most joyful tiding is the news of the good health and well-being of the

blessed, the exalted, the holy person of 'Abdu'l-
Bahá, 'He Whom God hath purposed'—may the
life of all created things be offered up for His
oneness.

9. A NUMBER of your spiritual sisters, namely
the handmaidens who have embraced His Cause,
have arrived here from Paris and the United States
on pilgrimage. They recently reached this blessed
and luminous Spot and have had the honour to
prostrate themselves at His Holy Threshold and to
behold the radiant face of 'Abdu'l-Bahá, the Centre
of the Covenant of Almighty God—may my life be
offered up as a sacrifice for His sake. We have now
the pleasure of their company and commune with
them in a spirit of utmost love and fellowship. They
all send loving greetings and salutations to you
through the language of the heart.

10. MAY the Light of Union radiate with greater
clearness and brilliancy day by day among the
people in your great country—for to this country
God has given much and much is expected from it.
But without harmony and love existing among
those who call themselves Bahá'ís, nothing will
be seen from it whatsoever; for verily the Believers

are the pivots upon which the fate of nations hang; and a difference among two believers is quite sufficient to consume and destroy a whole country. The one who works for harmony and union among the hearts of the people in these days will receive the greatest blessings and the most abundant bounties. There is no greater work for one to do upon this earth than to try and unite the hearts of the people—and especially those who are calling upon the Holy Name of God.

11. O MY dear sister! I have read what you wrote, and as I became aware of the content, I wept bitter tears. Then I carried the letter itself to 'Abdu'l-Bahá and He read it from beginning to end. These terrible events in Yazd call for cries and lamentation, and the shedding of tears of fire.

Although 'Alí's foes, on the plains of Karbilá, came as a rushing torrent of affliction against the Prince of Martyrs,[1] and even as ravening wolves, tore at the breasts of the favoured ones of the Court of Holiness, and wreaked their hate upon them and lifted their heads onto pikes—they leading out an expedition against the hapless victims, and carrying away all that these possessed—yet the span of that agony at Karbilá was but from the morning until noon, while the ordeal of the martyrs of Yazd lasted one entire month. And further, the companions of the Prince of Martyrs—may the souls of all those

[1] The Imám Ḥusayn.

killed on the holy Path be offered up for him!—made to defend themselves, and each one of them felled a number of those foes of 'Alí's House, spilled out the others' blood, before being martyred themselves. But these innocent victims of Yazd looked on their murderers with smiles, and gently welcomed them, and in exchange for the swords' blows offered honey and milk. Those set the blade to the victims' throats, but the martyrs presented them with sweets; those cursed and vilified them, while the martyrs implored God to forgive their murderers.

Although the slain on God's path at Karbilá were truly victims, helpless, innocent, so that the Concourse on High wept fiery tears over what the tyrants did in the desert there, still, we know that before every one of those great martyrs, some who battled against them fell down and died. But the martyrs of Yazd, at the onslaught of the foe, and under the tyrant's sword, uttered not even an unseemly word. . . .

Truly the harried survivors of these wronged ones have been subjected to the severest of ordeals, nor can any balm be found to soothe their wound, nor is there any antidote against this lethal drink. For them, every new morning is a new martyrdom.

Praise be to God, through the grace and favour of the Abhá Beauty—may all souls be offered up for those who are slain upon His path—the friends everywhere have arisen to do what they can for these survivors. But whatever we may do in such circumstances and however much we may sacrifice, it is still not enough, and they merit more. I hope that, with the confirmations of the Abhá Kingdom, we may be enabled to offer up our hearts and souls for the children of the martyrs, and think of ourselves as the servants of those noble ones.

12.   CONCERNING the remnants of the martyrs' families, you have mentioned how eager they are to hear a word of commendation assuring them that this act of self-sacrifice and martyrdom will be acceptable in the sight of God. Therefore, I mentioned this matter in His holy presence and I am glad to say that, in compliance with His instructions, a compilation containing most of the Tablets which have been revealed in honour of the martyrs of Yazd and elsewhere has been prepared. I am now sending it to you together with this letter. You may peruse these Tablets and then recite them in the presence of the remnants of those who have offered up their lives in the path of God, that they may be fully aware that those martyrs are well-favoured at the exalted threshold of the Almighty, and that the merciful glances of 'Abdu'l-Bahá—may our souls be His sacrifice—are at all times directed towards them.

On behalf of this bereaved and eager prisoner, convey loving greetings and salutations to all the handmaids of God there, particularly the remnants of the martyrs' families—and give them the joyful tidings that the memory of those dear souls, who have laid down their lives in the arena of sacrifice, has always been and will continue to be remembered at the fellowship meetings and in His holy presence.

13. O LEAF that has been stirred by the breeze of God! O victim of oppression in the path of the Abhá Beauty!—may my soul and the souls of the handmaids of God be offered up as a sacrifice for the dust of His Holy Shrine.

I earnestly hope that you may ever abide in peace and security within the shelter of the loving-kindness of the One true God, may labour diligently in those regions to serve His Cause and to diffuse the fragrance of holiness, that you may be confirmed at all times through His gracious assistance, and that, at the gatherings of the handmaids of God, you may shine forth as a bright candle, directing those loved ones of the Beauty of the All-Merciful to the path of divine guidance, exhorting them to be firm and steadfast, to be sanctified and detached so that they may, one and all, arise to fulfil that which is deemed worthy of these days, and by manifesting a goodly character and noble conduct cause that country to vie with the blissful Paradise.

14. ALL praise be to the Abhá Beauty, the Best-Beloved, the Desire of the world, for having enabled His well-assured leaves to remain firm in the Cause of God and steadfast in His love, even as immovable mountains, particularly the ladies belonging to the household of the Afnán—the twigs of the celestial Tree, who are resident in the land of Yá [Yazd]—upon them be the glory of the Most Glorious. In these days when tempestuous winds of tests are blowing and an ocean of trials has risen high, they have rid themselves of all earthly attachments, set their affection on the sacred beauty of the True One and have turned their hearts to the celestial kingdom.

The contents of your letter were highly appreciated. Praise be to God that from the rose-garden of its words and inner meanings the fragrance of spiritual fellowship was inhaled, and from the meadows of its pages the sweet melody of love, of remembrance and glorification of God was heard. It filled our hearts with immense joy, for it indicated that you were enjoying good health, and so were the saplings of the garden of God and the handmaids of the Merciful, particularly the remnants of the families of those who have offered up their lives in the path of the Lord of Mercy.

15. At the exalted Threshold of our Lord, the Best-Beloved of the world, I fervently beseech Him to graciously keep that assured leaf and the other handmaids of the Merciful safe and secure under the shelter of His bounty and grace.

The love-laden letter penned by that dearly-loved handmaid of God has reached this yearning prisoner and its perusal has filled my heart with joy and happiness, inasmuch as it indicates that you have turned in prayer and supplication to the Kingdom of God and been attracted to His divine fragrances. It imparted exceeding gladness and radiance, and thereby the hearts and spirits were inspired. Both at the sublime meetings convened in His presence and at the fellowship gatherings of the handmaids of the merciful Lord your name and the names of the beloved handmaids in India are often mentioned with high praise.

Praised be God that after attaining the holy Threshold of the Merciful in this hallowed land, this luminous Spot, you were able to take back with you the gift of the divine fragrance of holiness, to perfume the nostrils of the handmaids of God, to refresh and stimulate, nay rather revive and quicken the lifeless bodies through the potency of His wondrous exhortations, His sublime counsels and teachings. To all the handmaids of God announce the joyful tidings that both at the blessed and luminous Shrine and in the holy presence of Him Who is the Mystery of God we continually pray for all of you, extol your noble virtues, call to mind the memory of the radiant faces of those faithful leaves, and from the exalted court of the Lord of Glory implore for every one of you unbounded heavenly assistance and confirmation.

16.   ON my return from Beyrouth I was sorry to find out that you had left for Italy and I missed seeing you before you left. Not only I but all the holy household miss you very much. Though we miss you we are glad to learn that our Lord has directed you to go into the world and give the Glad Tidings of the Kingdom to the people and awaken the sleeping souls. How happy you must have been that you left with this thought in your mind that with the direction of our Lord you have gone. We hope that we soon will hear of your wonderful services in the Path of the Cause of God. Have no fear and be not down-hearted. Trust in Him. Be sure you will be successful at the end, for He has sent you and He will surely be with you and help you always.

17. O MY dear sister! Your excellent letter brought me much joy, testifying as it did to your ardour and pure intent, and to your being immersed in the ocean of God's heavenly love, and also to the harmony and concord among His handmaids —which indeed is the greatest of God's bestowals: for fellowship, closeness and love are glories of the Kingdom, and richest gifts from the Lord of dominion and might. We thank Him then for this great bounty.

To the honoured handmaid of God, Miss Barney, give my many and fond wishes. I implore God to assist her and yourself to attain the greatest of all His favours in His mighty Kingdom.

I conveyed the salutations from all of you, and your expressions of devoted servitude, to Him

Whom God hath purposed, the Centre of His ancient Covenant.

From this imprisoned handmaid.

18. THE Festival of Riḍván is come and the splendour of the light of God is shining from the invisible horizon of His mercy. The overflowing grace of the Lord of oneness is pouring down copiously from the unseen world and the glad-tidings of the Kingdom are coming in from all countries. The resplendent morn that betokens the advancement of the Cause of God and heralds the exaltation of His Word is dawning in every region.

Praise be to God that the fame of the Ancient Beauty—may my life be offered up for His loved ones—has been noised abroad in the world and the glory of His Cause is spread far and wide through-out the East and the West. These joyous develop-ments will indeed gladden the hearts of His loved ones.

19. YOU should not think that the record of those meetings can ever be blotted out from the pages of history or that the memory of those gatherings can fade from the face of the world. Nay every single act, every deed or utterance is a seed sown in the garden of life. Ere long it will grow and develop, yielding an abundant harvest even as a fruitful tree. . . .

Those sufferings were endured for the sake of God alone and for His love. They occurred during this century in which the Manifestation of God has appeared, and their underlying purpose was solely to glorify the Cause of the Abhá Beloved, and to exalt the Word of God. Indeed, a single deed performed in this Day is equivalent to the deeds of a thousand years.

20. BOTH in the Persian and Arabic Writings of the Primal Point—may the life of all men be offered up for Him—there are several, nay indeed numerous passages in which He directs His plea to the exalted court of Him Whom God shall make manifest, requesting Him to graciously protect the leaves of the Tree of the Bayán, that they may not fall away but rather attain their paradise which is the recognition of His Manifestation.

The detailed account you had given about the services she[1] has performed during the early days of the Faith is entirely true, and sufficient witness unto it is God. God willing, the services she has rendered and the hardships she has endured may yield excellent results. With the utmost humility and devotion we will pray for her at the Holy Shrine, beseeching divine confirmation and assistance. Likewise, in the sublime presence of Him Whom God has purposed we will beg earnestly for His tender solicitude and the outpouring of His special favours.

[1] Elsewhere in this letter reference is made to one of the female relatives of the recipient.

21. HIS HOLINESS ʿABDUʾL-BAHÁ ASCENDED TO
ABHÁ KINGDOM INFORM FRIENDS. GREATEST HOLY
LEAF.

22. NOW IS A PERIOD OF GREAT TESTS. THE FRIENDS
SHOULD BE FIRM AND UNITED IN DEFENDING THE
CAUSE. NAKEZEENS[1] STARTING ACTIVITIES THROUGH
PRESS AND OTHER CHANNELS ALL OVER THE WORLD.
SELECT COMMITTEE OF WISE COOL HEADS TO HANDLE
PRESS PROPAGANDA IN AMERICA. GREATEST HOLY LEAF.

23. MEMORIAL MEETING WORLD OVER JANUARY
SEVEN. MASTER LEFT FULL INSTRUCTIONS IN HIS WILL
AND TESTAMENT. TRANSLATION WILL BE SENT. INFORM
FRIENDS. GREATEST HOLY LEAF.

24. IN WILL SHOGHI EFFENDI APPOINTED GUAR-
DIAN OF CAUSE AND HEAD OF HOUSE OF JUSTICE.
INFORM AMERICAN FRIENDS. GREATEST HOLY LEAF.

25. THE hearts of the people of Bahá are
intensely burning by reason of the great calamity,
and their longing cries are rising up to the Concourse on High and the angelic dwellers in the
Abhá Paradise, yet, this day is the day of service,
and this time the time to spread the holy Teachings

[1] Covenant-breakers.

far and wide; therefore must God's loved ones like unto a shining flame, rise up to serve the Cause of God with all their might and vie with one another in service. Let them, even as shooting stars, drive the disloyal out—so that in the Preserved Tablet of God, they may be recorded with that company who ever stood faithful to His Covenant and Testament.

Shoghi Effendi, the Guardian of the Cause of God, the Chosen Branch and leader of the people of Bahá, as a result of intense and unceasing grief over this great bereavement, this supreme affliction, has determined to absent himself for a short period, in an effort to rest, and to regain his health, after which he will return to the Holy Land and resume his services and obligations to the Cause of God. During his absence, in accordance with his letter herewith enclosed,[1] this prisoner is appointed to administer the affairs of the Faith, in consultation with the members of the Holy Household.

For this reason I have temporarily made arrangements so that the persons named by Shoghi Effendi may meet and the affairs be conducted in consultation with them. It is my hope that during the period of his absence the beloved of the Lord and the handmaids of the Merciful will exert their efforts to advance the Cause and accelerate its growth. He is, verily, compassionate and merciful to His servants.

26.   WE thank you most sincerely for your kind letters of sympathy, and we appreciate your loving

[1] See III, 1, page 21.

Messages, which are as comforting balm to our wounded hearts.

It would be our wish to answer each letter individually, but the shock of our bereavement was so sudden, and the work to which we were compelled to attend, was so overwhelming, that time failed us. Now, we wish you to realize that your words of steadfast faith and love were our greatest solace throughout the days of our grief, for we felt that you would each and all faithfully and loyally strive to carry on the work for which the life of our Beloved Master was spent.

We are more than thankful to God that He has not left us without a leader, but that Shoghi Effendi is appointed to guide the administration of the Cause.

We hope that the friends of God, the beloved and the handmaidens of the Merciful, will pray for us, that we may be enabled to help Shoghi Effendi in every way in our power to accomplish the Mission entrusted to him.

27. REJOICED OVER CONVENTION NEWS. PRAYING FOR CONFIRMATION. HOLY LEAF.

28. IN this day, those holy souls are divinely confirmed who stand firm in the most sacred Cause of the Abhá Beauty, those who are steadfast, and loyal to the Covenant and Testament of 'Abdu'l-Bahá.

Praised be the undying glory of God that you and all His friends have attained this greatest of gifts. You stand fast-rooted in the divine Covenant, and you turn to the appointed Centre, the explicitly chosen Branch. In all the world, what conceivable bounty could ever be greater than this?

29. IT is not unknown to those who stand firm in the Covenant and Testament of God that the centre of violation and his associates, from the day of the ascension of the Ancient Beauty, may His Great Name be ever exalted, have been working night and day and continually putting forth all their efforts, to spread disorder and disrupt the Faith. At this time, because of our terrible affliction, the ascension of 'Abdu'l-Bahá—may the quintessence of our souls be sacrificed to His sacred resting-place—they are busying themselves more than ever with the circulation of false rumours and idle imaginings, their purpose being, one way or another, to instil doubts into the minds, and thus to achieve their vain and futile ends.

Alas for them, however, there is no doubt at all that they will achieve nothing but the failure of their plans and the frustration of their hopes. Utter disappointment and a bitter end is all they will ever gain—just as 'Abdu'l-Bahá—may our lives be sacrificed for His meekness—has foretold in His Will and Testament, where He clearly and unequivocally sets forth the dissidence, the mischief-making and the wicked designs of that abominable band. And it is certain that through the never-ceasing confirmations of God, the light diffused by the loyalty of the true believers will scatter the darkness of the suspicions which the malicious have been spreading, and the brightness that streams from the believers' faces will dispel the gloom of the people of doubt.

Briefly, for some time they had been applying to the various government agencies, in the hope that with the government's assistance they would be able to obtain legal support for their empty claims. However, God be praised, they were disappointed. Then came a day, Tuesday, January 30—that is, four months ago—when the disaffected gathered together at the Mansion of Bahjí, invited in some of the rabble of 'Akká, and after joint consultation, determined to go to the Holy Tomb, forcibly wrest its key from the caretakers, and hand it over to the arch Covenant-breaker, pivot of the violation. Such was the plan, the disgraceful action, devised by the prime mover of mischief and his lieutenant.

They then committed the brazen act. From the caretaker of the Holy Tomb, Áqá Siyyid Abu'l-Qásim, they took away the key by force, and he, unable to withstand their attack, at once dispatched his assistant, Áqá Khalíl, to Haifa, to report to Shoghi Effendi what had taken place. The news reached Haifa about two hours after sunset, and the matter was instantly referred to the Governor. On his stringent orders, the key was surrendered that very night and placed in Government custody until the matter could be fully investigated to determine the question of rightful ownership.

Now, after the passage of four months, the Government has rendered its verdict, to the effect that the question should be put to the Bahá'í community, and that whatever decision the Bahá'ís arrive at will be conclusive. If the Bahá'í community considers Mírzá Muḥammad-'Alí to be excommunicated, then he has no rights whatever to the takeover. Therefore, wherever Bahá'ís reside, they must, through the given city's Spiritual Assembly, and bearing the signature of named individuals who are members of the elected body, inform the British authorities in Jerusalem, either by cable or letter sent through His Majesty's ambassadors or consuls, that the Bahá'í community, in conformity with the explicit writings and the Will and Testament of His Eminence 'Abdu'l-Bahá, Sir 'Abbás Effendi, texts well known and available in His own hand—recognize His Eminence Shoghi Effendi as the one to whom all Bahá'ís must turn, and as the Guardian of the Cause of God, and that they have no connection whatever, either material or spiritual, with Mírzá Muḥammad-'Alí, whom they consider to be excommunicated from the Bahá'í Faith, according to the explicit writings of 'Abdu'l-Bahá.

It should be the request, therefore, of Bahá'ís of all countries, both men and women, in every important centre, wherever they may reside throughout the world, that the officials of His

Britannic Majesty's Government in Palestine, its Headquarters being Jerusalem, issue a categorical order that the key of the Holy Tomb—which is the Point of Adoration and the sanctuary of all Bahá'ís in the world—be restored to His Eminence Shoghi Effendi, the Chosen Branch, and in this way to render the Bahá'í community, whether of the East or of the West, more appreciative than ever of British justice. The text of both cable and letter, together with the address, have been written on a separate sheet, as enclosed. The message is to be signed by the representatives and known followers of the Bahá'í Faith in that city.

30. THIS dire calamity, this great affliction, the passing of 'Abdu'l-Bahá, may our lives be sacrificed for His meekness, has shaken us to the very depths. Our lives lie in ruins. In our hearts, the stars of happiness have set, the lamps of joy have been put out. No more, from the rose-garden of the All-Glorious, does the nightingale warble those songs that fed the spirit in days gone by. From over the flower-beds of Heaven, the dove trills and coos no more. Now is the bright morning dark, and blazing noon is night, and the sea of woe has surged, and a storm of sorrow has overwhelmed mankind.

Alas, alas, that luminous Moon, with His ravaged breast a thicket of arrows—darts of the evil-doers' taunts, their derision, their calumnies—and His heart grieved by the malevolence of His foes and the rebellion of the violators, is now hidden behind heavy clouds, has departed from this world's horizons, and has risen upward to the realm of transcendent glory, to the all-highest Horizon.

And now, at such a time as this, a time of our affliction and deep distress, the prime mover of mischief, the centre of sedition, thinking to profit by this eclipse of the Sun of the Covenant, the Moon of spiritual concord, has taken advantage of what he sees as a rare opportunity for himself, and has mounted a violent revolt, and with the support of their second chief, has begun to spread the most far-fetched of malicious accusations, and is busy day and night, stirring up trouble and carrying out plots and stratagems the details of which would take too long to enumerate here and which you will be informed of later on.

Although they behold in every instance only grievous abasement and disappointment, failures and defeats, still their burning jealousy blazes up within them all the more, and their haughtiness and arrogance only increase. At this hour of turmoil and deep anguish and sudden, unexpected calamity, our only consolation lies in service to the Cause of God, and steadfastness in His Faith, and the guarding of His Law, and in the bonds of unity among the friends, and their fervour and joy, and in deeds that exemplify the holy Teachings of the Abhá Beauty, may His name be exalted, and the counsels of 'Abdu'l-Bahá, may our souls be sacrificed for His servitude. It is our hope that we all shall be helped to achieve these things, which alone befit this sacred day.

It appears from your letter that you had written prior to the receipt of the Will and Testament of the Centre of the Covenant. You have certainly perused it by now. This Text is His decisive decree; it constitutes the very life of those endued with understanding. In it the Pen of Bounty has set forth in the most powerful, comprehensive, clear and detailed manner the obligations devolving on every stratum of the Bahá'í community, and has hacked out the tree of violation by its root, and has caused the centre of it to be forlorn and disgraced. He has specifically named the centre to whom all must turn, thus solidly fixing and establishing the foundations of the Covenant, and has clearly appointed the centre, to whom all the people of Bahá must direct themselves, the Chosen Branch, the Guardian of the Cause of God. This great bestowal is one of the special characteristics of this supreme Revelation, which of all Dispensations is the noblest and most excellent. Goodly be this to the steadfast, glad-tidings to the staunch, blessings to those who win the day.

Praise be to God, you have arisen to serve Him, and are actively teaching and spreading His Faith. Such a bounty merits thanks a thousand times over, and praises forever, in the hallowed sanctuary of the one Beloved.

Convey my Bahá'í salutations to all the faithful.

31. ALTHOUGH that supreme calamity, that great ordeal, the ascension of 'Abdu'l-Bahá, put the torch to the harvest of our hearts, and brought down both our outer and inner beings, wedding us to grief and ceaseless pain, yet praised be God, He Who is the Dayspring of the Covenant has appointed in writing a specific centre, and designated the Guardian of the Cause, Shoghi Effendi, as the one toward whom must turn all those who follow Bahá'u'lláh—His purpose being that the Faith of God and His Cause should remain secure and safe. For this greatest of gifts it is fitting that we should return a thousand thanks to the one Beloved, and offer a thousand praises to His court of holiness.

Likewise, the hand of divine grace has reared blessed souls who are shining today like lamps of guidance in the assemblage of the Company on High, and who like luminous stars are casting their bright rays across the skies of faithfulness. How often we heard the Master, the Centre of the Covenant, say: 'At the time when Christ rose out of this mortal world and ascended into the Eternal Kingdom, He had twelve disciples, and even of these, one was cast off. But because that handful of souls stood up, and with selflessness, devotion and detachment, resolved to spread His holy Teachings and to scatter abroad the sweet fragrances of God, disregarding the world and all its peoples, and because they utterly lost themselves in Christ—they succeeded, by the power of the spirit, in capturing the cities of men's hearts, so that the splendour of the one true God pervaded all the earth, and put the darkness of ignorance to flight.

'Now when I shall depart from this world, I shall leave more than fifty thousand blessed individuals, every one of whom is staunch and firm as the high mountains, shining out over the earth like sparkling stars. These are the quintessence of loyalty and fellowship and love. They are the self-sacrificing watchers over the Cause, and they are the guides to all who seek after truth. Judge from this what the future will be!'

It is certain that when we act in accordance with the Teachings of the Abhá Beauty and the counsels of 'Abdu'l-Bahá, then will this world become the Abhá Paradise, and its thorns and brambles of cruelty will change into a blossoming garden of the faithful.

May we all be enabled to achieve this end.

32.   O FAITHFUL servant of the Best-Beloved, the Most Glorious! O steadfast friend, flourishing in the garden of His luminous Beauty! The brief but informative letter you had written to Shoghi Effendi, the Chosen Branch, the Guardian of the Cause of God, has been received together with the scrolls of doubt you had enclosed. Indeed, men whose nostrils have been perfumed by the fragrance of the Abhá Paradise, whose ears have been exhilarated by the sweet melodies of the nightingale warbling in the rose-garden of immortality, and

whose souls have been refreshed and quickened by the reviving breaths of holiness, would surely be saddened to hear the screech of the raven and the croaking of the crow, and from them they would certainly endeavour to flee. For the disgusting odour of violation is like poisonous air, whose baneful effects upon the body and soul are injurious and harmful, nay rather it will eventually lead to terrible loss and perdition. Thus the way you have dealt with this matter is approved and acceptable.

Since Shoghi Effendi has gone on a journey for a while, this lowly one was prompted to answer your letter. Convey wondrous Abhá greetings to all the lovers of the Blessed Beauty and the faithful friends of 'Abdu'l-Bahá. And upon you be His glory.

33. O GOD, my God!

Thou seest me immersed in the depths of grief, drowned in my sorrow, my heart on fire with the agony of parting, my inmost self aflame with longing. Thou seest my tears streaming down, hearest my sighs rising up like smoke, my never-ceasing groans, my cries, my shouts that will not be stilled, the useless wailing of my heart.

For the sun of joy has set, has sunk below the horizon of this world, and in the hearts of the righteous the lights of courage and consolation have gone out. So grave this catastrophe, so dire this disaster, that the inner being crumbles away to dust, and the heart blazes up, and nothing remains save only despair and anguish.

Thou seest, O my God, in the midmost of this terrible event, this ultimate calamity, when the devoted never put aside their mourning dress, and the moaning and the tears never cease—how that malevolent band have, with all their powers, mounted an attack against Thy loved ones who are loyal to the Covenant, even as the assault of wolves upon the flock. They are striving, with all their strength, to bring down the mighty structure of Thy Covenant in ruins, and level Thy strong citadel to the ground, and turn away from Thy straight and clearly-marked path those Thou hast guided aright. O my Lord, I voice my complaint before Thee, and lay bare my griefs and sorrows, and supplicate at the door of Thy oneness, and whisper unto Thee, and weep and cry out.

O my kind Lord! Thou didst make a clear compact and a Covenant explicit and firm, not in veiled and allusive language, that all should turn unto the Centre of Thy Covenant and the Protector of Thy Cause—so that no doubts whatever would remain for the hostile and the suspicious to exploit; and then Thy lone Servant rose up to lift Thy banner high, and carry the day for Thy Faith. For thirty years He summoned the people unto Thee, publicly, privately, and spread Thy Teachings and Thy principles to every corner, every country of the earth. Night and day, He fostered Thy loved ones in the cradle of divine knowledge and wisdom, and endowed them with the qualities of the spirit. And all this time He bore, at the hands of that evil crew, not once but over and over again, every kind of outrage, and calumny, and oppression. For they were forever lying in wait for Him, were spying on Him at all times from their ambush, attacking Him in whatever manner they chose, swelling with their insolence and pride. And yet, through Thy strong support, Thine overwhelming confirmations, they were the losers in the end, and their strivings came to nothing in this world's life, and all they gained was their own ruin.

Then, O my Lord, Thou didst make Him to ascend unto Thee, to place Him at Thy side, and by this the pillars of joy were shaken to their base, and the hearts of the devoted were terrified, and the smoke of their sorrow overspread the earth. At such a time that hate-filled band, seeing their advantage in the dire event, came in from every highway and byway, advancing on every side to topple over the throne of Thy Covenant, and lead Thy loved ones to perdition. They have laid their very being in ruins and they know not. How far, how very far have they gone in their ignorance!

But the Centre of Thy complete and flawless Covenant, He Who occupies the seat of servitude to Thee in Thine exalted and all-glorious Cause, had written by Thy will and Thy power a Book that shall never be lost nor ever forgotten. Within it by Thy predestinating knowledge and might, He had set forth all that is essential and obligatory for the upraising of Thy Cause in this world below. It is a book in which all things are explained in minute detail, in such wise that no matters whether small or great have been left out. And by Thy will and pleasure He designated therein, in place of His own Person, a Branch grown out from the Tree of Thy holiness, one fresh and tender, verdant and flourishing, arising to serve Thee, dwelling in the groves of Thine eternity, and Thine immortal gardens. And he, after turning to Thy gracious countenance and through Thine ancient succour, is inviting the people unto Thee and unto Thy Covenant, sound and firmly-established, and is spreading Thy commandments and Thy doctrines throughout Thy land, and guiding Thy servants to the path that leads aright.

O my God, I beg of Thee by all the days which Thy Light, the Centre of Thy Covenant, did spend in scattering Thy sweet scents abroad, and by all the nights when that delicate and fragile Being rested not, but kept the long vigils, crying out unto Thee, expending His efforts to guard Thy Cause and Thy dear ones, exerting His utmost to spread out Thy bounties and bestowals—while the malevolent, comfortable against their pillows, rested in their beds—I entreat Thee, by the ordeals He endured, for the sake of exalting Thy Word, at the hands of those who join partners to God, and the deniers, and the deserters, to keep Thy loved ones safe from the arrows of the calumniators, and the doubts of those who mislead and betray. Hold them fast, then, in the gardens and groves of Thy Covenant and Testament, and make them to enter the pavilions of Thy good pleasure, and shelter them in the refuge of Thy protection, and cast upon them the glance of Thy mercy's eye, and guard them from deviation and schism. Make them to live in unity and harmony, one with the others, and aid them to serve Thy Faith and to spread Thy Teachings far and wide.

Verily Thou art the Living, the Eternal, the Watchful, the All-Powerful, the All-Knowing, the All-Wise.

O you true servants of the Holy Threshold, you faithful friends of 'Abdu'l-Bahá!

Our hearts are burning away with the intense emotions aroused by this most dreaded of calamities, and our souls are suffering the torments of this separation causing delay in correspondence with you, yet God be praised, you are all among the well-favoured at the divine Threshold, and are drinking from the winecup of the Eternal Covenant. To the holy summons, you have all replied 'Yea!'; you have seized the chalice of His Testament and held it high. You are enamoured of that world-adorning Face, your hearts are tightly bound to those curling locks, that waft the fragrance of the musk-deer's scent; you are held spellbound by that magic nature, and by the teachings like nectar on the tongue, refreshing the spirit; and all continually receiving divine bounties from the One alone beloved, and ministering at His Threshold, and sincere and pure of heart.

The glories of that Sun are shining now from out the high, immortal realms, and His glance is resting on His loved ones. The portals of everlasting blessings are opened wide. The succouring armies are standing ready, waiting to behold what efforts the loved ones will exert as they carry out the holy Will, as they boil up and roar like waves of the sea. Let them rest not for a moment, nor wish for quiet and repose; let them carry out all His behests and thus prove their loyal gratitude for all His endless grace.

Over a span of thirty years the Centre of God's Covenant rested not, nor was His human temple ever tranquil and at peace. By day, by night, He would be teaching and guiding stranger and friend alike, and protecting the Cause, and seeing to its progress, and for these things He sacrificed His life. Now does loyalty to Him require that the beloved should rise up in obedience to His instructions, and devote their efforts to teaching the Faith, and to passing around from one to the next this winecup tempered at the camphor fountain,[1] and to protecting God's Cause from the evil suggestions and the mischief of the adversary, and to guarding the structure of the holy Covenant from disruption at the hands of the Covenant-breakers. Now is the time to stand as an impregnable rampart around the city of the Cause of God, to defend it from the

[1] The word camphor derives from Arabic káfúr, as in Qur'án 76:5. Camphor has been used as a refreshing tonic in Eastern medicine.

assaults of alienation and violation, that come against it like Gog and Magog.[1]

Praised be God, those of His friends who have been cradled and fostered for many a year within His wisdom and His teachings, and have drunk deep from the soft-flowing waters of true and mystic knowledge, and whose eyes have been opened, whose ears are attentive, whose hearts are wise —these, in all that concerns faith and certitude and the abiding by His instructions, stand fixed and firm as the high mountains. They are even as the towering palm, the goodly tree 'its root firmly fixed, and its branches in the heavens.'[2] Their roots run deep, and the fruits they yield are sweet. They know a mirage for what it is; they know, too, what will endure—for 'As to the foam, it is quickly gone: and as to what is useful to man, it remaineth on the earth.'[3] They have heard and read of how the Covenant met with opposition and violation in the Dispensations of the past, and have both heard of and seen for themselves the storms of mischief and the tests that appeared in the early days of this Cause. They know how these trials are designed to sift and purify, and how the dense clouds of revolt and violation would gradually pass from its skies; for the errors and falsehoods of the violators can never

---

[1] cf. Qur'án 18:93: 'Verily, Gog and Magog waste this land . . .' The rampart here described was of iron and molten brass, so that Gog and Magog could neither scale it nor dig under it.

[2] Qur'án 14:29.

[3] Qur'án 13:18.

withstand the overwhelming power of the Covenant, nor can the mountains of diabolical suggestions ever stand under the rod of God's majesty and might.

O faithful loved ones of 'Abdu'l-Bahá! The centre of sedition, the focus of rebellion—whose evil character and passions, even in the days of the Ancient Beauty, made him known for his stubborn perversity and his ambition to lead—began to put forward certain claims, gathered about him a pitiful band, raised up the ensign of self-glorification and self-love, and considered himself to be a partner in authority with none other than Him Who was the True One, until in the end the hand of the Lord's omnipotence struck down his plans and hopes.

For a period of thirty years, he opposed the Centre of the Covenant and, to bring down His structure in ruins, did everything that lay in his power. This in spite of the fact that the divine Beauty had made His Covenant so strong, and appointed its Centre so explicitly, in writing, unmistakably, that He had left no room for any questions or doubts. In the Most Holy Book of Aqdas, which in this most excellent of all ages is the Mother Book, and embraces all, and again in the Kitáb-i-'Ahdí,[1] the last revealed Tablet by the Tongue of knowledge and wisdom, which contains the final wishes of God—the people of Bahá are directed with perfect clarity to turn their faces toward Him Whom God has purposed, and He is designated as the Interpreter of the Book,

[1] The Book of My Covenant.

the Resolver of all complex and difficult questions, and the Centre of the Faith. Therein as well are the other Branches, the Afnán and the rest of the believers bidden to direct themselves unto that One so that all might face one and the same Centre, and all be bound thereto. Thus would the basic foundation of God's Cause, which is unity, remain unassailable. Thus the root of heresy and rebellion would wither away, and just as in the days when He Who is the Truth was made manifest, so too in the day of His Covenant the light of unity would pervade all things, and put to flight the murk of disbelief and dualism and rebellion and opposition —and thus the tree of His holy Cause would grow and flourish, and the rich fruits borne by the holy Teachings would satisfy all needs and be sweet in the mouth of all mankind.

This fact of there being only one Centre and of turning unto a single holy Being is, in the Kingdom of His Cause, as the shaft or spindle of a millstone, and all the other laws and ordinances must needs revolve around this one. In the temple of God's religion the Centre of the Cause can be likened to the heart, for upon it depends the life of the human body as one entity, as well as the relationships of its organs and their essential growth and vitality. In human society the Centre of the Cause can be compared to the sun, whose magnetic force controls the movements and orbits of the planets. The Centre of the Cause is also like the spine of a book, for by it the pages are all banded together into one book, and without the spine the papers would become loose and scattered.

Now each separate member of the community who is within the shelter of that blessed unity is, according to his rank and station, the recipient of grace; and that rank is respected and protected, in conformity with the verse: 'Not one of us but hath his clearly designated station.'[1] Thus, in the body of man, the eye has a preordained station, one not belonging to some lesser members; and yet, should it once depart from the whole, and its connection with the centre be broken, then its membership in the body, and its very life, are ended, let alone its previous station and degree. Or should the eye be plucked from its place, torn out of the body, it would be deprived of life itself, how much less would it continue to enjoy the station that rightly belongs to the eye.

How strange! With reference to one who smokes opium, the Ancient Beauty, the Most Great Name, has said: 'He is not of Me', making no distinction here between one enjoying God's special favour, and some other. If the smoking of opium, which is one of the secondary and lesser prohibitions, completely severs the smoker from membership in the community and from relationship to the Person of the Manifestation, then what must be the condition of him who refuses to acknowledge the Centre of the holy Covenant? In the words of Christ, 'If thine eye

[1] Qur'án 37:164.

cause thee to stumble, pluck it out . . . if thy hand offend thee, cut if off . . .'[1]

O would that they had contented themselves with their refusal to recognize that shining Being —with their failure to obey Him and to be lowly before Him. But no, they beat upon rebellion's drum, and hoisted the flag of contumacy and spite, and blew the trumpet of calumnies across the world. In the hearts of the credulous they sowed seeds of disaffection, and inconstancy and opposition. They made common cause with the hostile, the biased, the mockers, who were arrayed against the Faith of the Blessed Beauty, flattering them and paying them bribes and holding out promises and hopes; they worked hand in glove with those occupying the seats of the judiciary, and those authorized to interpret the law and pronounce judgment, and those who sat on despots' thrones, and with still others who were engaged in affairs remote from God's; and by all manner of deceits and stratagems incited them to utterly extirpate the Covenant of Almighty God and the Centre of it. They even, with a liberal distribution of funds, hired assassins to shed the sacred blood of that Vicegerent of the Glorious Lord.

Could any just person imagine that such as these have any relationship or spiritual connection whatever with the Beauty of the One true God, or that they could be accounted as members of the

[1] cf. *Matthew* 18:8–9; *Mark* 9:43–7.

Bahá'í community? Would not such as these be only plucked-out eyes and palsied hands?

⁕ Look at the treatise that their second chief wrote, regarding their first chief and his associates—in which he described, with his own pen, in minute detail, their shameful purposes and actions relative to the Centre of the divine Covenant —aims and acts that no perverse and godless tyrant would consider permissible treatment for anyone. Their second chief tells how, to a despotic and oppressive government, they brought false and malicious accusations against 'Abdu'l-Bahá; how they undertook to uproot the holy Tree; how they forged Tablets, in Bahá'u'lláh's name, that denounced the Centre of His Covenant; how they altered and corrupted the holy Texts to such a degree that he said his confidence in the reliability of the holy Tablets was virtually shattered.[1] These and their other shameless activities are all set forth; and strangest of all is this,

[1] On p. 14 of 'An Epistle to the Bahai World' written by Mírzá Badí'u'lláh, translated by Dr Amínu'lláh Faríd, and published by the Bahá'í Publishing Society in Chicago in 1907, there is the following passage concerning the falsification by Muhammad-'Alí of a Tablet in which Bahá'u'lláh relates the misdeeds of Mírzá Yahyá, to whom He refers as 'My brother'. Mírzá Badí'u'lláh writes: 'A few moments passed and I saw him [Muhammad-'Alí] take up the Tablet, erase "My brother" and replace it with "My Greatest Branch". Having seen this, I immediately said: "This deed is a great sin and a breach of trust. If you show this Tablet, this servant will divulge the whole account, will point out the interpolation, and this will cause all the writings in your possession to be considered unreliable.

that he, their second chief—the very one who wrote the confession so full of the abominable acts of their first chief and his associates—now cleaves to the first one like flesh to bone.

They are setting the axe to the root of the Cause of God; nor are they in the least ashamed, nor put to the blush, before the Lord God and His watchful and perceptive servants. There even exists a paper in the hand of Shu'á', son of their first chief, in which he tells of a person who was commissioned and was ready and waiting to martyr the Centre of the Covenant.

> If I my tale could tell,
> No bounds my pen would know;
> My work would swell,
> My book will grow,
> For tons of scroll
> Would bear my woe.

For over a period of thirty years, always increasing their efforts, they inflicted extreme anguish on 'Abdu'l-Bahá; and they did not, in all this span, ever take one step nor draw a single breath to help the Faith. They spent their entire time in attempts to wean the beloved of God away from obedience to the Centre of the Covenant, and to undermine their

Hereafter whatsoever of the writings traced by the Supreme Pen you may show me, I will not accept as authentic until I have carefully compared the manuscript with the original handwriting which is elsewhere preserved and have examined the same with a magnifying glass.''

convictions, making them waver in their faith, and turning them cold; and because of what they did, thousands of souls were veiled from the holy Cause, and prevented from embracing it.

Such then is a glimpse of their aims and actions, which made them to be cut off from the Holy Tree, and excluded them from glory and joy everlasting. They lost out, both here and hereafter, and 'this verily is utter perdition'.[1]

O you men who stand fast and firm, you women who are steadfast and firm in your faith! Whensoever I visit the Holy Shrines, I think of you, and in all lowliness at His Threshold, I entreat the Almighty to send down upon you all His invisible confirmations, and to let His endless bounties enwrap each one of you—so that through the efforts of those chosen ones of God, the lights of loyalty and sincerity and truth, and staunchness in the divine Covenant, will be shed upon that town;[2] that it may be delivered from the consequences of ill-omened disaffection and violation, and that instead, a fortunate star may rise there out of the concealing depths and mount upward to the heavens; that no scrolls of doubt, and of calumnies against the divine Covenant, may remain therein; and that every name there may be written down in the heavenly register of those who have kept the faith.

O Lord, set their feet firm in Thy Covenant; let them hold fast to the cord of steadfastness in Thy

---

[1] Qur'án 22:11.
[2] Khúsif.

Cause. Protect them from the hosts of discord and calumny, and cause them to come under the sheltering banner of Thy Testament, that is raised high on the summits of the earth.

Light up then in their hearts the flame of severance from everything except Thy love, and help them by Thine overwhelming might to labour for Thy Teachings.

Verily Thou art the Generous. Verily Thou art He Whose bounty embraceth all things.

May the lights and the splendours be shed upon all of you.

34. To the doves of faithfulness, ever since that most grievous of disasters, the passing of 'Abdu'l-Bahá, this world of dust has become a cage, and a place of torment; and to the unrestrained nightingales it is only a prison, narrow and dark.

Certainly, a pure soul will not bind his heart to this passing show, and the gems of spiritual love will yearn only to be let go, out of this world. Nevertheless, the all-compelling will of God and His all-encompassing and irresistible purpose has desired that this dark earth should become as the Abhá Kingdom, and this heap of dust be changed until it becomes the envy of the rose gardens of Heaven.

This is why the Manifestations of God, the Day-springs of that all-glorious Sun, have willingly accepted to bear, and take upon Their own sacred and immaculate Selves, every trial and tribulation

and calamity and hurt. And They have established
laws and ordinances, that assure the flourishing and
freedom and joy and salvation of all the human race.
In this way that primal purpose will be revealed, and
that subtle mystery divulged.

Thus too, have They trained certain souls, and
reared them with the hands of loving-kindness, that
these should arise to perform the noble and exalted
task, and should devote their efforts toward carrying out this duty, watering the Tree of life and
serving all mankind.

Praise be to God, you are confirmed and
flourishing in the Faith, and partaking of your
portion from that heavenly table, and are receiving
your benefits in both worlds.

35.   THE passing of 'Abdu'l-Bahá, may our lives
be a sacrifice for His meekness, was the ultimate
calamity, the most great disaster. The light has fled
our hearts, and our souls are wedded to sorrow, and
no power in all the world can furnish any consolation, save only the power that comes from the
steadfastness of the believers and their deep-rooted
faith, and their unity, and their love for one another.

Only these can lessen the pain and quiet the
anguish.

Although to outward seeming the Sun of the
Covenant has hidden Himself behind the clouds,
and the Orb of the Testament is concealed, and on
the holy horizon of glory, He has now set, and is lost

to view—still His rays are shining from out His hidden place, and forever will His light shed down its splendours.

For ever and ever will He, with all that invisible grace, and those bestowals of the spirit, lead the seeker onward, and guide the yearning, and ravish the hearts of the lovers.

The Will and Testament of 'Abdu'l-Bahá is His decisive decree; it gathers the believers together; it preserves their unity; it ensures the protection of the Faith of God. It designates a specific Centre, irrefutably and in writing establishing Shoghi Effendi as Guardian of the Faith and Chosen Branch, so that his name is recorded in the Preserved Tablet, by the fingers of grace and bounty. How grateful should we be that such a bounty was bestowed, and such a favour granted.

Now is the time to arise to serve the Faith with all our might, that our loyalty may be clearly proven, and that we may perfectly, to the fullest extent and in minutest detail, carry out the requirements of self-sacrifice. It is my hope that one and all, we shall succeed in this.

36.   THE ascension of Him Who was the Temple of the Covenant, the setting of Him Who was the Orb of harmony, 'Abdu'l-Bahá, may our lives be sacrificed for the wrongs He suffered, was the most dire calamity, and the most dread of ordeals. It dissolved our very hearts, it laid low the very pillars

of our being. It made our eyes to shed tears of blood, and our sighs and the sound of our weeping reached upward to the Concourse on High. Then did a sea of anguish roll up great waves of grief, and a whirlwind of sorrow swept over the peoples of the earth.

That blessed soul, following the ascension of the sacred Abhá Beauty, may our lives be sacrificed for the dust of His sacred threshold, and until the hour when His own luminous spirit rose up to the realms on high, for a period of thirty years had neither a peaceful day nor a night of quiet rest. Singly and alone, He set about to reform the world, and to educate and refine its peoples. He invited all manner of beings to enter the Kingdom of God; He watered the Tree of the Faith; He guarded the celestial Lote-Tree from the tempest; He defeated the foes of the Faith, and He frustrated the hopes of the malevolent; and always vigilant, He protected God's Cause and defended His Law.

That subtle and mysterious Being, that Essence of eternal glory, underwent trials and sorrows all the days of His life. He was made the target of every calumny and malicious accusation, by foes both without and within. His lot, in all His life, was to be wronged, and be subjected to toil, to pain and grief. Under these conditions, the one and only solace of His sacred heart was to hear good news of the progress of the Faith, and the proclaiming of God's Word, and the spreading of the holy Teachings, and the unity and fervour of the friends, and the staunchness of His loved ones. This news would bring smiles to His countenance; this was the joy of His precious heart.

Meanwhile He trained a number of the faithful and reared them with the hands of His grace, and rectified their character and behaviour, and adorned them with the excellence of the favoured angels of Heaven—that they might arise today with a new spirit, and stand forth with wondrous power, and confront the forces of idle fancy, and scatter the troops upon troops of darkness with the blazing light of long endurance and high resolve; that they might shine out even as lighted candles, and moth-like, flutter so close about the lamp of the Faith as to scorch their wings.

The Will and Testament of 'Abdu'l-Bahá, may our souls be sacrificed for His meekness, is our guiding light upon the path, it is the very bounty of the Abhá Kingdom. This Text is the decisive decree, the way that leads aright, the highest hope of all who stand firm in the Covenant of the Lord of Lords. It is tidings of great joy; it is the ultimate bestowal.

37. WE rejoiced greatly to learn of the unity among the friends, their staunchness, their ardour, and the fact that they have established a Spiritual Assembly. It is clear that the stronger grow the bonds of yearning love among the believers, and the fiercer its fire, the more will they find themselves embraced by the bounties of the Ancient of Days,

and receiving the continuous confirmations of the Greatest Name. Thus will the Assemblies of the friends become reflections of the gardens of the Concourse on High, mirroring forth the radiance of the Abhá Kingdom.

From Their supernal realms and Their immortal heights, He the exalted Báb, and He Who is the Beauty of the All-Glorious, and the wondrous presence of 'Abdu'l-Bahá, all These are gazing down upon Their faithful loved ones, beholding what they do under all conditions, their behaviour and conduct, and all their words and ways, waiting to cry 'Well done!' when They see the Teachings carried out, and 'Blessed art thou!' to whoso may excel in doing the bidding of his Lord.

Those divine, those sacred and exalted Beings bore every grief, and They accepted tyranny from every traitor, to make an Abhá Paradise out of this dust heap of the world, and change this place of thorns and sorrows into blossoming bowers of love. They trained Their loved ones, and fostered them with the hands of grace, and sent them forth, with countless treasures, with goodly gifts, and with the forces of Heaven massed behind them—that they might become guides, and holy cup-bearers, of the living, soft-flowing waters of divine bestowals.

God be thanked, the believers in that country are confirmed and blessed, and have arisen to serve the Cause, and are straining every nerve to spread the heavenly Teachings far and wide. They are faithful ministers at the Holy Shrine of the Blessed Beauty,

and true lovers at the sacred Threshold of
'Abdu'l-Bahá.

38. THAT supreme affliction, the passing of
'Abdu'l-Bahá, was the direst of ordeals; it was an
anguish of mourning. The parting with mankind's
Beloved set fire to the hearts of all His lovers, and the
souls of the believers dissolved in its burning. Even
the beauteous dwellers in the Abhá Paradise cried
out and wept, and in their empyrean abode the
Maids of Heaven moaned and lamented. The gems
of holiness fell a prey to crushing grief, the essences
of sanctity bowed down in sorrow.

That One whom the world has wronged could
rest neither day nor night. From moment to
moment, at the hands of every betrayer, yet another
cruel arrow was shot into His heart, and ever and
again, from one or another assailant, He was
calumny's target. In the dark of the night, out of the
depths of His bosom, could be heard His burning
sighs, and when the day broke, the wondrous music
of His prayers would rise up to the denizens of the
realm on high.

That Prisoner, grievously wronged, would hide
His pain, and keep His wounds from view. In the
depths of calamity He would smile, and even
when enduring the direst of afflictions He would
comfort the hearts. Although He was hemmed
about with disasters, and living at the whirlwind's
core of grief, He would still proclaim the Cause of

God, and protect the Holy Faith, and He brought God's Word to the ears of those in East and West. He trained and nurtured friends of such a kind that whensoever their names were on His lips or spoken in His presence, His blessed face would glow and His whole being would radiate with joy. Many and many a time He would express His trust and confidence. In the gatherings held toward the close of His days, He would repeatedly tell of the apostles of Jesus. Among other things He would say that when the Spirit[1] left this nether world and hastened away to the glorious Kingdom, He had but twelve disciples, and even of these, one was cast off; and that this small number, because they sacrificed all they had for Jesus, and immersed themselves in the radiance of that sweet and comely Being, and lost themselves in Christ, they lit the world. 'Now when I depart,' He would say, 'I have loyal loved ones that number 50,000 or more, and each one of these is a mighty fortress to guard the edifice of God, each one, for the Ark of the Faith, is strong as armour-plate. They are rooted firm as the high mountains, they are bright and rising stars, they are jewels, they are pearls.' Today, God be thanked, these qualities are radiating from the faces of the righteous, and shining upon their brows.

That blessed Being perfected His bounties for the people of Bahá, and His grace and favour were extended to those of all degrees. In the best of ways, he manifested at the end what had been shown forth

[1] Jesus.

at the beginning, crowning all His gifts with His Will and Testament, in which He clearly made known the obligations devolving upon every stratum of the believers, in language most consummate, comprehensive and sound, setting down with His own pen the name of Shoghi Effendi, as Guardian of the Cause and interpreter of the Holy Writ. The first of His bounties was the light He shed, the last of His gifts was that He unravelled the secrets by lifting the veil.

God be praised, all the beloved of God's Beauty are immersed in an ocean of bounty and grace, all are receiving abundant bestowals from the lights that radiate from that Countenance of glory.

39. THE good news that the Word of God is being raised up, and His Cause glorified, and that His friends, on fire with love for Him, are arising to spread His sweet savours abroad—is coming in steadily from every quarter of the globe.

All are firmly rooted in the Faith, steadfast, turning with complete devotion to him who is the appointed and designated Centre, the Guardian of the Cause of God, the Chosen Branch, His Eminence Shoghi Effendi; are founding Assemblies, conducting meetings, teaching most eloquently and with all their energies, presenting proofs, disseminating the doctrines of the Divine Beauty and the counsels of 'Abdu'l-Bahá. It is certain that ere long the light of these Teachings will illumine the earth and gladden the hearts of the people of Bahá.

40. ALL the virtues of humankind are summed up in the one word 'steadfastness', if we but act according to its laws. It draws to us as by a magnet the blessings and bestowals of Heaven, if we but rise up according to the obligations it implies.

God be praised, the house of the heart is lit by the light of unswerving constancy, and the soul's lodging is bedecked with the ornament of faithfulness.

Steadfastness is a treasure that makes a man so rich as to have no need of the world or any person or any thing that is therein. Constancy is a special joy, that leads us mortals on to lofty heights, great progress, and the winning of the perfections of Heaven. All praise be to the Beloved's holy court, for granting this most wondrous grace to His faithful people, and to His favoured ones, this best of gifts.

41. IT is clear how that most dire of calamities, that most great disaster which was the ascension of 'Abdu'l-Bahá, may our souls be sacrificed for His meekness, has set our hearts on fire and dissolved our very limbs and members in grief. Darkness settled on our souls, of blood were our tears. Even the essences of sanctity cried out in fear, and the gems of holiness moaned and lamented, while our

own inner selves fell to ashes, and there was no peace left in the soul, no patience in the heart.

No more does the ardent nightingale carol its joyous songs, and the sweet and holy melodies of the immortal dove are hushed. That gleaming Moon is hidden now behind the clouds of everlasting life, that Orb of the high heavens sank down at the setting point of glory and rose into the skies of the world that we see not, and above the realm of the placeless He is casting forth His rays.

With His departure, these afflicted ones were plunged into a sea of pain, and beaten and blown about in a whirlwind of anguish more violent than the spoken or the written word can tell. Our days wear away in tears, our nights in sighing, and it is this storm of grief and regret and yearning that has kept us from writing before now, even to send you our love.

It is certain that the people of Bahá, who are the dwellers of the Crimson Ark and breast the seas of the Lord, and who have attained to the bounties of the Abhá realm, and who are steadfast in the Covenant —they, men and women alike, young and old alike, share with these homeless ones the anguish of our bereavement and this direst of ordeals. We could hear, with the ear of the spirit, the wailing of those lovers of Him Who was the Ravisher of hearts, those like us scorched by the fires of separation, and from our own sad hearts we would lift our cries of sorrow to the heavens, and weeping would send up our entreaties in such words as these, to the threshold of the luminous Beauty of God:

O kind Lord! O Comforter of anguished hearts!

Send down Thy mercy upon us, and Thy grace, bestow upon us patience, give us the strength to endure. With Thy generous hand, lay Thou a balm upon our sores, grant us a medicine for this never-healing woe. Console Thou Thy loved ones, comfort Thy friends and handmaids, heal Thou our wounded breasts, and with Thy bounty's remedy, restore our festering hearts.

With the gentle breeze of Thy compassion, make fresh and green again these boughs, withered by autumn blasts; restore Thou to flourishing life these flowers, shrivelled by the blight of bereavement.

With tidings of the Abhá Paradise, wed Thou our souls to joy, and rejoice Thou our spirits with heartening voices from the dwellers in the realm of glory.

Thou art the Bounteous, Thou art the Clement; Thou art the Bestower, the Loving.

From the first dawning of the new light, that noble land shone with the rays of the Great Announcement, and was lit by the sunbeams of the Ancient Beauty. Like heavy rains, the bounties beat upon that sacred place, and out of clouds of mercy, grace showered down upon that region of resplendence, bringing freshness and new greenery, and the trees of being then turned verdant, and there burst forth blossoms of the spirit, and wind-flowers of true knowledge blew, and mystic myrtles grew and flourished. And from out of that land came musk-laden gales, scenting with their perfume the other lands as well, and scattering far and wide the musk-deer sweetness of heavenly mysteries.

So it was that Khurásán became the grove of the lions of God, and a nesting-place for the birds of the Riḍván Paradise. The Ancient Beauty singled out that blessed land for special favour, extending to it uncounted blessings and gifts. Now in wondrous and most sweet voice, again with the tracings of His exalted pen, and on the head of each one of the beloved in that bright region, He set a crown of imperishable glory, and He robed each one with His bestowals and grace, and wrapped each one in a mantle of spiritual perfections. Of them all He spoke the highest praise, and to all He gave abundant blessings, as is proved by the text of His scrolls and Tablets. And whenever that sacred King of all the world would speak of Khurásán, His being would stir for joy, and His luminous face would grow still brighter with exceeding gladness. His bounties never ceased, and from clouds of grace His favours continually showered down upon that land.

Then came the era of the Covenant, and that full cup was passed from hand to hand, and the Sun of the Covenant rose up, shedding abroad on the horizon of unity the rays of servitude and thraldom, and lighting up the hearts of humankind. New life was breathed into the body of the world, and into the human soul came a fresh measure of delight. The hearts of the people of Bahá rejoiced to hear the glad-tidings from the Abhá Kingdom, and the minds of those who had sought shelter under the

Tree of holiness were illumined with beams of
fidelity and faith. Once again, the loved ones in that
region were inebriated with the wine of the Primal
Covenant, and in their firmness and steadfastness
and loyalty they led the field. They showed forth
such constancy as to astonish the mind, and they
manifested such power and endurance as to raze the
piled-up doubts of the doubters to the ground. Of
the poisoned winds of violation there was no trace
left in all that land. The hopes of the disaffected were
blighted, and the centre of violation clearly witnessed the defeat of all his aims and plans.

It is certain that those who have caught the
fragrance blowing from the Abhá Paradise, those
who have heard the nightingale singing from the
immortal gardens and taken delight therein, those
who have trembled for joy, and whose souls have
been renewed when the breezes of holiness out of the
bowers of the All-Merciful were wafted over them
—will find the raven's croaking and cawing a
wearisome thing, and can only turn from it and flee
away.

For thirty long years, from the hour of
Bahá'u'lláh's ascension until His own immaculate
spirit passed into the light of the all-highest realm,
'Abdu'l-Bahá rested neither night nor day. Single
and alone, a prisoner, a victim of tyranny, He rose
up to reform the world—to refine and train and
educate the human race. He watered the tree of the
Faith, He sheltered it from the whirlwind and the
lightning bolt, He protected God's holy Cause, He

guarded the divine law, He defeated its adversaries, He frustrated the hopes of those who wished it ill.

All His life long, that quintessence of eternal glory, that subtle and mysterious Being, was subjected to trials and ordeals. He was the target of every calumny, of every false accusation, from enemies both without and within. To be a victim of oppression was His lot in this world's life, and all He knew of it was toil and pain. In the dark of the night, He would sigh out His grief, and as He chanted His prayers at the hour of dawn, that wondrous voice of His would rise up to the inmates of Heaven.

Under such conditions, He trained and with His own hand fostered a number of souls who would stand as a mighty fortress protecting the Cause, and as armour-plate for the Ark of the Covenant. With awesome power, these would scatter the forces of illusion, and with heavy blows, strike down the false rumours of the people of doubt. God be praised, that labour bore fruit, and the meaning of those toilsome efforts became plain. Those blessed souls rose up in all their loyalty, and with their steadfastness and long-suffering they served as shining examples for the children of salvation.

His bounties, His favours to the people of Bahá were made perfect, and extended to every class and kind. And as at the beginning, so at the end: His final bestowal of all, a crowning adornment, was His Will and Testament. Here, to Bahá'ís of every degree, in the clearest, most complete, most unmistakable of utterances, He described the obligation of each one, explicitly appointed, irrefutably and in writing, the Centre of the Faith, designating the Guardian of the Cause and the interpreter of the Holy Book, His Eminence Shoghi Effendi, appointing him, the Chosen Branch, as the one toward whom all must turn. Thus He closed for all time the doors of contention and strife, and in the best of ways and in a most perfect method He pointed out the path that leads aright.

Thus by its very roots He pulled out the tree of mischief and dissension. He razed the structure of violation to the ground. He left no margin for error, no room for doubts. And thus He crowned the first of all His loving-kindnesses with this last of them. Let us praise and thank God for this supreme gift, this great bounty.

Following that disaster of His passing, that dire ordeal, Shoghi Effendi, the Guardian of the Cause, was overwhelmed by such never-ending grief and by his now heavy burden and supreme responsibility, that his sensitive heart could bear it no more. And so, after making the necessary arrangements, he sent out a letter expressing his wish to be alone for a time, in a quiet and secluded place, away from the noise and turmoil of everyday life—there to pray and supplicate and urgently beg for help from the realm of the All-Glorious.

With this in mind, he has gone on a journey, leaving us to loneliness and grief. Our hope is that very soon, the good results of this journey will become apparent, and that the friends will rejoice to see the important benefits that it will yield; that he will soon come home, and that once again correspondence with him can be resumed, and the doors of access will be opened wide.

42. ALL praise to the omnipotent Lord, that in this auspicious day He Who is the Sun of bounty has shone out so fair and bright as to light up the world of the hearts. He has burned away the veils of waywardness and ignorance. He has struck off the fetters of baseless myths and ignoble concepts that chained the people hand and foot. He has cleansed and burnished the mirrors of men's souls, sullied by the dust and rust of this dark world. He has opened wide the door to that Celestial Tavern of matchless wine, and He is freely pouring out the immortal draught of knowledge and perception and love. He has hoisted the banner of oneness, and destroyed the foundations of estrangement. Under the sway of His unity, the many-coloured races and diverse religions have tasted the rose-red wine of His love, and are aliens no more. Those pure in spirit who have set eyes upon Him, and approached the place He dwells in, reflecting Him have shone out like mirrors, and cleaving to Him alone, they have detached their hearts from all else but Him. They have heard, with their inner ears, His words, and they have noted His ways, and forgotten all else. They are ever soaring upward, out of the lower

world to the world above, and they are fit to be told the mysteries, and they understand them.

Such a day, then, is a day for praise and thanks, a time of benedictions and blessings, a time to wash away the stains of earth's defilement.

Let us turn our hearts to the world aloft, and cup our hands and supplicate our matchless Loved One, and urgently entreat Him, saying:

O Thou Kind Bestower, O Nourisher of our souls and hearts!

We have no aim, except to walk Thy path; we have no wish, except to bring Thee joy. Our souls are united, and our hearts are welded, each to each. In offering Thee our thanks and praise, in following Thy ways and soaring in Thy skies, we are all one.

We are helpless, stand Thou by us, and give us strength.

Thou art the Protector, the Provider, the Kind.

43.   INDEED, you have adorned yourself with the qualifications of faithfulness and are striving to fulfil the requirements of servitude to the Abhá Threshold. You have been inebriated with the wine of the love of God, have quaffed your fill at the banquet of loyalty to His Faith and have caused the seekers of truth, those that are sore athirst for the life-giving waters of His grace, to drink from the heavenly stream of true understanding. This was indeed most fitting and appropriate. For in this grievous calamity, this distressing bereavement, the

Bahíyyih <u>Kh</u>ánum, *circa* 1890

Bahíyyih <u>Kh</u>ánum, October 1919

Bahíyyih Khánum, an early photograph

Facsimile of Bahíyyih Khánum's handwriting (*for translation see p. 95*) best consolation and solace that the spiritual souls could offer is to dedicate themselves to the service of the Cause, to diffuse widely the sweet savours of holiness, to become wanderers in the path of that heavenly Best-Beloved, to let their whole beings burn and melt, and be enkindled with the fire of His love. Such indeed is the effective remedy, the most potent cure for this irreparable agony, for this aching of the heart and soul. There is no other remedy.

Praise be to God that the effusions of celestial aid from the Abhá Kingdom are unceasing and the outpourings of heavenly grace from the Concourse on High uninterrupted. You should not think that your memory may ever, even for a moment, be removed from the minds of these oppressed ones, or that your remembrance may fade from the hearts of these exiled servants. The Abhá Beauty bears me witness and 'Abdu'l-Bahá is my testimony that no word can possibly express how indissoluble are the ties of spiritual communion and fellowship that bind us to the loved ones of God and to the handmaids of the Merciful.

44. THE deep heart's love and the longing of the soul of this wronged one for those spiritual beloved ones, and in particular for those who are kin to the peerless Holy Tree of sanctity and oneness, cannot be told in words, and my most ardent wish is that I might correspond with each one of you, but our alarm and grief over this momentous happening,

this terrible affliction and ill-omened agony, this in-
exorable divine decree, the passing of 'Abdu'l-
Bahá—may our souls be offered up for all the
wrongs He bore!—has left us wretched, deso-
late, to such a degree that there is no peace in the
spirit, no will to endure in the heart.

This is an earthquake which shook the foundations of our lives, this is a wailing and an uproar
within the Company on High. The lightning bolt of
this departure has set the very world aflame, and the
fires of this leave-taking have scorched the whole
earth.

The grieving dwellers in the courts of holiness
have rent their garments of long-suffering, and the
household of the Most High have put on mourning
dress. Truly the people of Bahá and those who are
kin to the divine Lote-Tree are sharing with us the
pangs of this bereavement, this direst of torments,
and are partners in anguish of those who suffer here.

Now that this dread event has come upon us all, it
is to be hoped that new stirrings and wondrous new
vibrations will be felt; that a renewed staunchness
and fidelity, an ever more vigorous firmness and
loyalty, will take over and astound the world. Thus
all will clearly understand that even though that
sacred and mysterious Being has laid aside the
garment of His mortal life, even though that Bird of
eternity has abandoned the cage of this earth, still is
His spirit in our midst, still is He watching over us
all from the realm of the All-Glorious, ever is He
gladdening the hearts of the beloved, and to the

souls of those who are fast-rooted in the Covenant, ever is He bringing tidings of great joy.

45. THE good news has come that the Will and Testament of 'Abdu'l-Bahá, may our lives be sacrificed for His meekness, has been read at the meetings of the friends, and we here are rejoiced to learn of their unity and their steadfastness and loyalty, and of their directing themselves toward the designated Centre, the named and specified Guardian of the Cause of God, the interpreter of the Book of God, the protector of His Faith, the keeper of His Law, Shoghi Effendi. This news brought extreme joy.

It is certain that enlightened and sensitive minds and spiritual hearts will continually obtain illumination from the Centre of Mysteries, and beg for bounties in abundance from Him Who is the Celestial Beauty Unconstrained. The ear of their intellect is hearkening to the divine call from the Company on High, and they drink the draught of faithfulness from bounty's cup. To them, all that is not the Beloved is nothing at all, and from whatever is not the good-pleasure of God, they veil their eyes. They worship truth, they seek reality, and they are intoxicated with the wine of His love.

God be praised, you have attained these bestowals. Now is the time for zeal and ardour, the season of fervour and joy. Thoughts must be focused on one Centre, opinions united on a single point, to publish abroad the Teachings of God and to act in

accord with the counsels of 'Abdu'l-Bahá, so that
the light of divine confirmations may wax ever
brighter, and the bounties of divine favour and
success appear on every side, and that in a brief
period, great progress will be made, and secrets now
hidden will be divulged, and joy and radiance will
appear.

It is to be hoped that out of the concealed and
manifest favour of the Abhá Beauty, He will
generate a new spirit in His loyal loved ones, and
make them to radiate a new and wondrous joy. This
indeed does not seem far from the outpourings of
His bounties and bestowals.

46. IN this noblest of all ages the Sun of grace
and loving-kindness has shone out from the divine
day-spring with such resplendent glory and is casting
His beams so bright and far, that He has lit up all the
earth and made the hearts and minds of men to be as
sanctified mirrors and reflectors of holiness—this to
such a degree that from turning their faces unto that
bright Orb, that Star of the loftiest heaven, those
illumined beings have received abundant grace and
have been enabled to understand the secret of God's
oneness, and the mystery of His unity, and to
become alert to subtle realities.

Praised be God the Beloved that He has disclosed,
through His invisible bounties and visible grace,
such secrets, and drawn such veils aside. Words have
taken on new meaning, and meaning itself has been
adorned with the divine. A clear Covenant makes

our duty plain; an explicit and lucid Text explains the revealed Book; a specifically named Centre has been designated, toward whom all must turn, and the pronouncement of him who is the Guardian of the Cause and the interpreter of the Book has been made the decisive decree. All this is out of the grace and favour of our Beloved, the All-Glorious, and the loving-kindness of Him from the splendours of Whose servitude earth and heaven were illumined.

'Abdu'l-Bahá, may our lives be sacrificed for His meekness, has filled to overflowing the cup of bounty for the people of Bahá, and encompassed with His grace persons of every degree. He has destroyed the very basis of disunity, ruined any attempts at dissension and mischief, and clearly pointed out to all the highway of guidance, now and for evermore.

The hope is that we may arise with a new spirit and be confirmed with bountiful blessings, and urge on our steeds in the field of service, of purity and sincerity, and of high endeavour—nor is this much to ask of the loving-kindness and grace of our exalted Lord.

47. THE purport of your letter is highly indicative of your steadfastness in His Cause, of your unswerving constancy in the Covenant, of having set your face toward Shoghi Effendi, the authorized Point to whom all must turn, the Centre of the Cause, the Chosen Branch, the bough that has branched out from the twin heavenly Trees. Indeed, this is the

essential thing, this is the meaning of true devotion, this is the unshakable, the indubitable truth whereby the people of Bahá, the dwellers of the Crimson Ark, are distinguished.

The loved ones of the All-Merciful are those that have truly served the Most Exalted One,[1] have been nurtured by the hand of the Abhá Beauty, have received training under the care of 'Abdu'l-Bahá —may our life be sacrificed for the wrongs suffered by Them. Such souls have drunk from the soft-flowing river of true understanding, have quaffed their fill from the living waters of assurance, have set their affection on the one true God, and have rid themselves of all attachment to aught except Him. They tread the straight path of truth and stride along His undeviating way. They incline their attentive ears to the Call of the Concourse on High and are attracted to the Celestial Voice ringing from the realms of glory. Great indeed is their blessedness, and may they meet with a good ending.

We earnestly hope that through the bounty of the Lord of eternity a fresh measure of His confirmations may soon appear and you may be encompassed by His pervasive aid and assistance.

48.   At this hour while yet the heart burns with the anguish of sorrow, and the gloom of bereavement still hangs low, my thoughts turn in loving remembrance to my sincere beloved sisters and brothers in the Cause.

[1] The Báb.

The news of your firmness in the Covenant, of your endeavour to work in unity and harmony, and of your untiring zeal and devotion in the Path of Service, has been a source of untold joy to me. For now my sole comfort lies in the loyalty and faithfulness of the friends, and my one joy in the progress of the Cause.

Dear friends! At this critical time through which the Cause is passing the responsibility that has fallen on every individual Bahá'í is great, and his duties are pressing and manifold. Now that the Sun of the Covenant has set on the horizon of the world, the eyes of all the people are turned expectant upon us. Now the time has come for the faithful friends of 'Abdu'l-Bahá, who have been the recipients of the Glorious Light, to shine forth even as brilliant stars. The radiance of our Faith must be such as to dispel the clouds of doubt and guide the world to the Day-spring of Truth.

Our firmness must be such as to cause him who wavers and errs to turn back penitent unto the fold; our unity and love must be such as to cause the peoples of the world to join hands in amity and brotherhood; and our activity in service must be such as to have all parts of the world resound with the echoes of 'YÁ-BAHÁ'U'L-ABHÁ!'.

For inspiration and guidance let us turn unto His life-imparting exhortations: '*O friends, show forth your fidelity! O my loved ones, manifest your steadfastness and your constancy! O ye who invoke His Name, turn ye and hold fast unto Him! O ye who lift up your hearts and implore His aid, cling to Him and walk in His ways! It is incumbent upon every one of us to encourage each other, to exert our utmost endeavour to diffuse His divine fragrances and engage in exalting His Word. We must, at all times, be stirred by the breeze that bloweth from the rose-garden of His loving-kindness, and be perfumed with the fragrances of the mystic flowers of His grace.'*

Thus does 'Abdu'l-Bahá still call to us from His realm of effulgent glory. Will not each of us hearken unto His voice, and exert the utmost endeavour to fulfil His hopes?

Dear friends, this is the day of faithfulness; this is the day of unity; this is the day of service. Let us not wait, nor ponder, but, detached from the world and its concerns, clad in the armour of faith, filled with the divine spirit of love, and quickened by His life-giving exhortations, let us arise in utmost love and harmony, hasten to the field of service, and subdue the domain of hearts with the arms of the love of God and the sword of peace and brotherhood.

For all inspiration and assurance let us turn unto Bahá'u'lláh's promise: *'Be not dismayed, O peoples of the world, when the day-star of My beauty is set, and the heaven of My tabernacle is concealed from your eyes. Arise to further My Cause, and to exalt My Word amongst men. We are with you at all times, and shall strengthen you through the power of truth. We are truly almighty.'*

Dear friends! A great obligation of every Bahá'í

is vigilance to protect and shield the stronghold of the Faith from the onslaught of the enemies. In these days their activity has waxed strong. They are constantly on the alert, and exert the utmost endeavour to cause such harm as would impede the onward march of the Cause.

Association with such people will cause discord and unrest among the friends and will be detrimental to the progress of the Cause. Therefore it is urgent that the friends exercise great wisdom and vigilance lest through the evil schemes of the enemies a breach be made in the Faith. The few people whom 'Abdu'l-Bahá pronounced as injurious to the Cause must be shunned by all the friends, as Shoghi Effendi himself tells us to do in his second letter to the American believers.

49. O STEADFAST ones, gathered beneath the Abhá Beauty's standard of oneness, O faithful lovers of 'Abdu'l-Bahá! Sad news has come to us out of Iran in recent days, and it has intensely grieved the entire Bahá'í world: they have, in most parts of that land, set bonfires of envy and malevolence, and hoisted the banner of aggression against this much-wronged community; they have left no means untried, no plot or strategy neglected, and have arisen with extreme hostility and spite to pull out by their very roots the trees of this garden of God.

From every side, they are aiming their arrows at hearts that rejoice in the knowledge of God and are filled with the love of Him. From every ambush, they are hunting down gazelles that pasture in the meadows of His unity. They are taking the men and women believers captive, and making orphans of the children. They are plundering the believers' property, sacking their hearths and homes.

Those, however, who have been trained and educated in the school of God, even when coming to such a pass, are resignation itself, and to the brutal aggressor they are as the living waters of Heaven. They are rivers of pure mercy and peace. Though powerful and well able to defend themselves, they never raise a hand to strike, nor do they open their lips to protest. They confront the others' taunts and curses with prayers that God will forgive them, and their reply to the wounds of bullet and sword is to offer milk and honey. They kiss the murderer's hand; as intoxicated lovers, they drain the martyr's cup.

Such is the way of those who are attracted to His Kingdom, and that other is the behaviour of the foolish, the heedless of God. So has it been, at the time when the Manifestations of God appeared: the heedless and the ignorant turned upon their heavenly Teachers, and the diseased harried and tortured their loving Physicians in the spirit, idly thinking that they were acquiring merit thereby. Thus have their imaginings always been, at the outset of every Faith: that by such cruel acts they could destroy that seed, the Word of God; or that by blowing against it, they could put out the lamp that

He has lit; or that by directing a storm of denial against them, they could bring down His trees, so flourishing, so firmly rooted in His Kingdom, or lay His fair gardens in ruins.

But as, time and again, experience has shown, in every age they have only seen verified the Blessed Beauty's assurance that calamity's rushing rain is the greening of His planted field, and afflictions are the oil that feeds and adds to the radiance of the lamp of God. And then, as the days go by, and they see with their own eyes the Day-Star in its noonday splendour. witness the bewildering richness of the fields that God has sown, behold His great and all-pervading Cause—then the fires of hatred and envy flame out of the hell of their natures; they can contain themselves no longer, and the truth of the holy words is proved, that God will not bring down a people from their station unless they have corrupted their good qualities themselves, and it becomes clearly shown that God brings on the downfall of the heedless little by little and in ways that they know not.

During occurrences of this kind, it is incumbent upon the believers in other countries to immediately adopt prudent and reasonable measures, that through wise methods such fires may be put out. Let them not allow the claws of ravening wolves to be reddened with their brothers' blood; let them defend God's lambs from the hungry leopard's knife-sharp teeth; let them guard the members of the one and single Bahá'í family from the poisoned sting of scorpions and snakes.

This is the unique obligation of the Bahá'ís of the world. Addressing the believers, Bahá'u'lláh says: 'Be ye as the fingers of one hand, the members of one body.' This means that just as each member safeguards the rest, warding off any threatened harm, so too must the individual Bahá'ís do, whether in the East or the West. At this time it is urgently needful, and it is the request of this grieving servant, that the assembly of the believers in that area act at once, and take the case to the ambassador of the Iranian government. Let them tell him, 'The holy Cause of Bahá'u'lláh has so unified us who are His world-wide followers, and has brought us so close together, that we have become like a single body. If the foot of a Bahá'í, in the farthest Eastern land, is so much as scratched by a thorn, it is even as if we Bahá'ís here in the West had suffered the same. We have now received word from Írán that in Shíráz, in Sulṭánábád, in Hamadán, in Káshán, even in Ṭihrán, and in other places as well, the fanaticism of the ignorant and heedless has been fanned into flame, and that agitators are stirring up the populace—with the result that our brothers and sisters, who are but well-wishers of all human-kind and are indeed the world's only hope for peace, and are obedient and helpful citizens of Iran and her government, find themselves under attack and pushed into the heart of the fire.

'We therefore request the representative of Iran to ask his government to safeguard our brothers in Iran from the aggressions of their enemies, and to deliver that flock of God's lovers from the claws of the wolf, and provide for their security and well-being. By bringing us word of this outcome, Írán will earn the deep and heartfelt gratitude of thousands of Bahá'ís who reside in these countries, and widespread appreciation will be voiced by us in our many gatherings, of her government's good offices on our behalf.'

And further, if it be possible, you should make this same representation through your own ambassador in Ṭihrán, so that he may direct the attention of the Iranian authorities to these persecutions, and awaken that government to the possibility of divine retribution and to the shameful stigma occasioned by such actions directed against this innocent community by the heedless and ignorant amongst the mass of the people.

Let him make them aware that there are thousands of adherents of this Faith of the love of God around the world, who are gazing in astonishment and disbelief at the savage acts now being perpetrated against their brothers, and are eagerly waiting to hear that the government has come to the rescue of this unique, this law-abiding people, who are the well-wishers of mankind, from the attacks of the ravening wolves.

I pray for you continually at the Holy Threshold, and call upon Him on behalf of each one of you, and beg that He will bestow on you the blessings of the Kingdom.

Upon you, men and women alike, be the Glory of the All-Glorious.

50. A PHYSICIAN treats every illness with a certain remedy and to every painful sore he applies a specially prepared compound. The more severe the illness, the more potent must be the remedy, so that the treatment may prove effective and the illness cured. Now consider, when the divine Physician[1] determined to conceal His countenance from the gaze of men and take His flight to the Abhá Kingdom, He knew in advance what a violent shock, what a tremendous impact, the effect of this devastating blow would have upon His beloved friends and devoted lovers. Therefore He prepared a highly potent remedy and compounded a unique and incomparable cure—a cure most exquisite, most glorious, most excellent, most powerful, most perfect, and most consummate. And through the movement of His Pen of eternal bounty He recorded in His weighty and inviolable Testament the name of Shoghi Effendi —the bough that has grown from the two offshoots of the celestial glory, the branch that has branched from the two hallowed and sacred Lote-Trees. Then He winged His flight to the Concourse on High and to the luminous horizon. Now it devolves upon every well-assured and devoted friend, every firm and enkindled believer enraptured by His love, to drink this healing remedy at one draught, so that the agony of bereavement may be somewhat alleviated and the bitter anguish of separation dissipated. This calls

[1] 'Abdu'l-Bahá.

for efforts to serve the Cause, to diffuse the sweet savours of God, to manifest selflessness, consecration and self-sacrifice in our labours in His Path.

51. I WAS very glad to know of your meeting with the Chinese students, and I am sure your effect and influence shall be great upon them because their fresh and receptive minds are ready to grasp the importance of this Manifestation; and when you go to China, which you may if you think it wise, your influence and success, I hope, will be still more.

I pray God that He should confirm you in your teaching, and when you go to China, He should make you a pioneer in carrying the Message of this Dispensation to the farthermost countries of the world and to the most obscure.

The members of the Holy Family join me in extending to you their love and Bahá'í greetings, and may the spirit of 'Abdu'l-Bahá guide you and keep you.

52. WE were delighted to receive your excellent letter . . . and read it with joy. It gladdens our hearts to witness from its contents the evidences of loyalty and sincerity and perfect steadfastness in the Cause of God, and unshakeable constancy in His Covenant.

I offered praise to my Lord, the All-Glorious, for His abundant blessings, the prodigality of His bestowals, and His wondrous grace; for He has created such spiritual beings, such illumined essences, who attract bounty from the Sun of Truth, and are lit by its heavenly light, which unravels the mysteries, parts the curtains, and tears aside the veils. He has sent forth pure and holy souls whom the blame of the blamer cannot shut out from the Faith of God, nor frighten away from establishing the truth of His Teachings. These are they whose thirst is quenched, whose ills are healed, whose hearts are gladdened, whose minds are set at rest, whose souls are stirred, whose spirits rejoice, whose eyes find consolation by beholding the splendours of the beauty, and the graces of perfection, that come down, one following after another, from the firmament of glory. Well is it with them for such wondrous gifts, and bliss be to them for such blessings!

As for me, acquainted with great grief as I am, subjected as I am to calamities, I have no solace in this dire ordeal that has suddenly come upon me to darken my days, save only to see happiness in the hearts of the believers; to breathe in the sweet scents of loving-kindness from the gardens of their hearts, and to behold the sparkling lights of unity amongst God's chosen ones, and to note how widespread are the breaths of fellow-feeling and love amongst the righteous, and how His teachings and the Will and Testament of 'Abdu'l-Bahá are being disseminated throughout those lands—always in accord with wisdom, as enjoined by the Almighty and set forth in the Writings.

I beg of God, even as a pauper, and I implore Him with all lowliness, feebleness and contrition, to assist you all with His unseen favours, and open before your eyes the portals of His bounty and grace, and make ready for you whatsoever you desire out of His everlasting bestowals, and make all things easy for you, and fulfil your hopes—so that in serving the Faith of your Lord, the Glory of the All-Glorious, you will reach your furthermost goals. Verily is He the Almighty, the Ever-Forgiving.

I beg of Him too, that He will cause every difficulty to vanish away, and will dispel every cloud, until it becomes possible for you to present yourselves at this blessed, this luminous and fragrant Spot, and bow down your foreheads in the dust of this bright Threshold, and attain this ultimate goal, for the friends long to behold you.

Again, I supplicate the Eternal Glory to send down His herald of holiness with the garment in his hands,[1] that all eyes may be solaced and all hearts rejoiced by the return to this country of the Chosen Branch, the Guardian of the Cause of God, Shoghi Effendi, in the briefest of times. This indeed is well within the reach of the bounties of our Almighty and All-Generous Lord.

53.   FOLLOWING the ascension of 'Abdu'l-Bahá to the Abhá Kingdom the only thing that can afford

[1] See Qur'án 12:93.

consolation to the heart of this grief-stricken and wronged maidservant is to see the lovers of that luminous Countenance happy, joyful and radiant and to behold the diffusion of the sweet savours of God, the exaltation of His Word, and the growth of His Faith. Nothing else matters.

The duty of the concourse of the faithful in this day should be but one duty, their purpose but one purpose, their aim but one aim, and the object of their endeavour but one object, and this is none other than to foster the spirit of unity and harmony, to serve and teach His Cause and to promote His Word. Such is the meaning of true faithfulness; and in this lies the good-pleasure of 'Abdu'l-Bahá.

54. THE letter that you wrote in your burning grief, on the passing of the world's Beloved, the Orb of the Covenant—wrote with weeping eyes and a heart afire, has come. Once again, it brings back the full force of this calamity, and renews our mourning. This was the most ruinous of disasters, the most dreaded of ordeals, the most hurtful of misfortunes. It was an earthquake that shook the pillars of the world; it caused a tumult and an uproar among the dwellers of earth and heaven. This terrible separation came upon us as an inescapable trial and a dismal decree. It destroyed all hopes of happiness, and all joy perished. By this departure, the sparkling stars were dimmed, and the heavens of mystic meaning split apart. It set the skies on fire, it

scorched the seven spheres. From this departure, sorrow enveloped all mankind, it brought pain and tears to all the peoples of the earth. The lightning bolt of it consumed the world and struck the hearts of its inhabitants, so that they put on sackcloth and poured ashes on their heads. This disaster, coming all unawares, made the morning dark, and turned bright noon to night. From our breasts rose burning sighs, and from our eyes streamed our life blood. Even the Concourse on High moaned and lamented, and their clamour rose to the highest Heaven, and the weeping denizens of the pavilions of glory, striking at their faces, raised their plaintive cries. Mourning, shedding tears, their garments rent, their heads uncovered, their feet bare, the Maids of Heaven hastened out of their lofty, immaculate chambers, and groaned and cried out.

'Abdu'l-Bahá, may our lives be sacrificed for His sacred dust, that peerless Beloved of the world, from the day that Bahá'u'lláh ascended until the hour of His own spotless soul's departure to the kingdom of light and the realm beyond, had neither a quiet night's rest nor a peaceful day, for thirty years. At all times His heart wept and sorrowed, and in the dark of the night from His anguished breast rose burning sighs, sorely wounded as He was by the arrows of the opposers and the rebellious. Then at first light, He would lift up His wondrous, melodious voice and commune with the dwellers in the high mansions of Heaven.

He would face the storms of tribulation with a

heart full of fervour and love; He would breast the waves of calamities and oncoming ordeals with overflowing joy. With the balm of His loving-kindness, He would remedy unhealing wounds, and the medicine of His unending grace was a cure for mortal ills. Through His tenderness and care the sorrowful found comfort, and through His Words the despairing received the blissful consolation of their incomparable Lord. He would hearten the despised and the rejected with outpourings of grace.

In the pathway of Bahá'u'lláh, He made His holy breast a shield to bear adversities, made His beauteous face a target for the blows that rained upon Him from all sides. He, the Wronged One of the world, was compassed about by rebel hosts; the armies of treachery assailed Him from every direction. The disaffected were not remiss in their cruelty and aggression; never once did that arrogant crew fail to spread a calumny or to show their opposition and their malice. At every moment, they inflicted wounds upon Him, injured Him, brought fresh grief to His heart. Their sole aim was to bring down the structure of the Holy Faith and to destroy its very base and foundation. They did all in their power to split the Bahá'í community, and in their strivings to shatter the union of the believers, they neglected nothing. They joined hands with every enemy of the Faith, became boon companions of all who betrayed it. There was no mischief, no plot, no slander, no aspersion, that they would not allow themselves, no individual so vile that they would not cleave to him.

And thus, with all His own ordeals and cares, and banished from His home, He Whom the world wronged devoted Himself to counselling and nurturing the people with the utmost loving-kindness, divinely admonishing them, leading and guiding them at all times to complete and utter steadfastness in the Cause of God.

From one direction He would ward off the assaults of the nations, from another He would hold back the people of hatred from tormenting the believers. Now He would scatter the waverers' clouds of doubt, again He would demonstrate the truth of the clear and manifest Verses, and at all times and seasons He would guard the Cause of God with His very life, and protect its Law.

His fundamental purpose in enduring that continual toil and pain, and bearing those calamities, was to safeguard the divine and all-embracing Word, to shelter the tree of unity, to educate persons of capacity, to refine those who were pure in heart, and to transform the hearts of the receptive, to expound the mysteries of God and illumine the minds of the spiritual.

All praise be to Bahá'u'lláh! The meaning of those bounties became apparent and the splendour of those bestowals was made manifest: that conclusive Text, the Will and Testament of 'Abdu'l-Bahá, was given us, and what had been hidden at the

beginning was made known at the end. His infinite
grace became clearly manifest, and with His own
mighty pen He made a perfect Covenant, naming
Shoghi Effendi the Chosen Branch and Guardian
of the Faith. Thus, by God's bounty, what had been
a concealed mystery and a well-guarded secret, was
at last made plain.

This greatest of bestowals came as a lightning-
flash of glory to the righteous, but to those evil ones
who broke the Covenant, it was the thunderbolt of
God's avenging wrath.

55. ALTHOUGH the ascension of the beloved
Centre of the Covenant was the ultimate calamity,
the severest of ordeals, and the fire of that bereavement consumed our hearts and souls, and there were
no eyes but wept their tears of blood to mourn Him,
no breast but uttered fiery sighs—still, God be
praised, the Will and Testament of that Wellspring
of bounty and grace, and the designation by Him of
the Centre of the Faith and of the Covenant, quieted
our burning grief and stilled our sighing, and came
as balm to our sorely-wounded hearts.

The power of the Faith prevailed, the awesome
majesty of the Word of God flashed out, and day by
day reveals in increasing measure its overpowering
might.

And now, to offer gratitude befitting such a
bounty, we must prepare ourselves, gird ourselves
for service, and rise up and live in accordance with
the instructions of the Blessed Beauty and the

counsels of 'Abdu'l-Bahá, for these are the life of the world and the salvation of its peoples. Thus, from every direction, will the portals of happiness and spirituality open before us all.

The Chosen Branch, the Guardian of the Cause of God, Shoghi Effendi, because of the intense grief and suffering and pain inflicted by this terrible event, has desired to spend a period alone, in a quiet spot, where he can devote his time to prayer and supplication, and communion with God. He, therefore, left us sometime ago, but our hopes are high that in a very short time he will come home to the Holy Land. For the moment, then, this wronged and sad one has answered, however briefly, the letter from your distinguished Assembly.

56.   YOU have offered up thanks to the Lord for appointing the Centre of His Cause and the Guardian of His Covenant, and have voiced your gratitude and expressed your spiritual sentiments, for this favour and grace.

It is true, in all the world there could be no mercy greater than this, no bounty more abundant.

'Abdu'l-Bahá, may our lives be sacrificed for His sacred dust, has bestowed on us a wondrous gift, a most great favour. He has clearly shown us the highway of guidance and explicitly designated the Centre toward whom all the people of Bahá must turn, and with His own bounteous pen has written

down for us what will ensure prosperity and progress, and salvation and bliss, for evermore.

Now is the time to arise and serve with all our
powers, that we may grow happier day by day, and
fill our hearts with warmth and joy.

57. THE Ancient Beauty, the Most Great Name,
has, through the splendours of His grace in this most
glorious of all ages, made this world of dust to
radiate light. The loving counsels of 'Abdu'l-Bahá
have turned the beloved of the Lord into signs and
tokens of humility and lowliness. He has taught
them selflessness, and freedom from material
things, and detachment from the world, and has
enabled them to understand the verities of Heaven.

In that supernal realm we are all but motes; in the
court of the Lord God's majesty we are but helpless
shadows. He is the Shelter for all; He is the Protector
of all; He is the Helper of all; He is the Preserver of
all. Whensoever we look upon ourselves, we, one
and all, despair; but He, with all His grace, His
bestowals, His bounties, is the close Companion of
each one.

It is certain that tests and trials are inseparable
from this life and a vital requirement thereof,
especially for the human race and above all for those
who claim to have faith and love. Only through
trials can the genuine be known from the worthless,
and purity from pollution, and the real from the
false. The meaning of the sacred verse: 'Do men

think when they say 'We believe' they shall be let alone and not be put to proof?'[1] prevails at all times and is applicable at every breath, and fire will only bring out the brightness of the gold.

So it is my hope that with lowliness and a contrite heart, with supplications and prayers, with good intentions and faithfulness, with purity of heart and adherence to the truth, with rising up to serve and with the blessings and confirmations of the Lord, we may come into a realm, and arrive at a condition, where we shall live under His overshadowing mercy, and His helping hand shall come to our aid and succour.

58. AFTER the construction of the Báb's Shrine on Mount Carmel, it was the wish and intention of 'Abdu'l-Bahá—may our lives be sacrificed for His holy dust—to open a path that would lead directly from the Shrine to the German Avenue. Time and again He referred to this project and explained how it should be built. You are no doubt familiar with this matter. However, in those days many obstacles stood in the way, preventing the execution of this important project. Among them was a house located at the beginning of this path at the foot of the mountain, which belonged to one of the German settlers. This house had become a serious barrier, inasmuch as the owner had turned down every offer for the purchase of the property. The German

[1] Qur'án 29:2.

community had adopted a policy in the administration of the real estate within the boundary of their settlement which required them not to sell any tract of land or any house within that area to outsiders, no matter how lucrative the payment might be. This ruling was strictly observed by them and had developed into an insurmountable barrier. Another obstacle was that the projected path would pass through tracts of land which belonged to different people, and some of them were unable to sell their property due to legal problems, while others deliberately would not sell since they had perceived that this path was exclusively intended for access to the Bahá'í Shrine and that the Bahá'ís would eventually be compelled, no matter when, to pay an enormous sum for the acquisition of this land. Thus immersed in the sea of visionary hopes and dreams they categorically refused to sell. So days and nights, and months and years passed by until the hand of divine power wrought a change in the whole situation, and the truth of the words: 'He shall establish His ascendancy over His dominion as He pleaseth' was fulfilled; for not long afterwards this territory was occupied by the equitable Government of Great Britain, and the local authorities, acting according to their own judgement, decided that the existence of the above house in that locality was undesirable. Therefore they demolished the house, cleared the site and carried away the stones. Then the Municipal Engineer prepared a design for the path, emphasizing that the opening of that path to the

Bahá'í Shrine was imperative. This design received the blessed attention of 'Abdu'l-Bahá Who graciously approved it and expressed His satisfaction and appreciation to the Municipal Engineer. Later on, with the aid of divine confirmations, enough land was purchased from the remaining tracts through which the path passed.

59. AT the Threshold of the Lord of Mercy we supplicate Him to grant perception and understanding to the ignorant, to awaken and bestow awareness upon those who are fast asleep and to give the eye of insight to the men of authority who conduct the affairs of the people, so that they may clearly distinguish the peace-maker from the mischief-maker, the faithful from the traitor, and the well-wisher from the ill-wisher.

60. THE adherents of the Faith of Bahá'u'lláh have, under all circumstances throughout the past sixty years or more, clearly proved themselves to be the well-wishers of all governments and peoples and have demonstrated that they are lovers of peace, are sincere, trustworthy and devoted. However, they often become the object of calumny and slander uttered by some foolish people. Indeed, such has ever been the way of God.

From time immemorial even to this day the chosen ones of God have always been exposed to the woes and sufferings that the disdainful have inflicted upon them. They have been made the targets of the darts and spears of hatred and enmity that the heedless have unloosed upon them. Yet it is clear and evident that the loved ones of God will always, with the whole affection of their hearts and souls, welcome every tribulation in the path of the peerless Beloved and will, with utmost joy and love, accept the pain of every grievous wound for the sake of the incomparable One. Far from grieving or complaining, they offer praise and thanksgiving to Him Who is the Sovereign Lord of all. They commit their affairs to the care of the Lord of all mankind and surrender everything to Him Whose power is irresistible. He is the Potent, the Powerful, the Avenger, the All-Compelling.

61. REGARDING the Centre of Sedition[1] and his scrolls of doubt, this individual, for a period of thirty years, both within and without the Cause, was busy with his mischief-making, and planting his seeds of contention and dissension. He had in mind but one concern, one single thought: to create discord in the Faith. All this is well known to everyone, it is clear as the noonday sun, and is set forth in the Writings of the Centre of the Covenant, including His Will and Testament,

[1] Muḥammad-'Alí.

where this person's evil intentions, satanic plots and diabolic acts are a matter of record, and there is no need to elaborate on them here.

So things were until recent times, when we were subjected to this direst of all ordeals. Once again, the Centre of Sedition, believing that the field was his, and seizing the occasion, rose up and began to spread abroad his scrolls of doubt, heedless of the fact that the instructions and commandments of the Blessed Beauty, may His Name be glorified, and the counsels of 'Abdu'l-Bahá, may our souls be sacrificed for His meekness, had reinforced the base of the Cause, and firmly established the edifice of the Word of God, and They had, through God's favour and grace, drawn Their faithful loved ones into a realm where no power in all the world, nor the awesome majesty nor the onslaughts of the world's embattled armies, could so much as disturb the faith of a single Bahá'í child, nor make him to stray from the path that leads aright. How much less could such as he affect those noble personages every one of whom is rooted firm in the love of God, and stands immovable as the high mountains!

God be praised, during all these long years, all this individual ever achieved was injury to himself, and the defeat of his plans, and the disappointment of his hopes. Nor will he ever have anything more.

In recent times, especially, from whatever direction he mounted his attack, he discovered a solid barrier that proved impossible to assail, and found his slings and arrows of doubt turned back against himself. Thus were fulfilled the words of 'Abdu'l-Bahá in His Will and Testament, that 'The Centre of Sedition was ... confounded in his craftiness ...' To whatsoever place this person addressed his evil treatises of doubt, these same treatises were sent straight back to him, some with a reply, some without, and thus he found it hopeless to make a breach in the Cause of God.

62. YOUR letter has come, and I myself and the Holy Family were infinitely grieved to learn of the sufferings you have undergone, being made as you were the targets of such injustice, malevolence and aggression.

Since, however, you stood firm and steadfast and unchanging, as the arrows of tyranny came against you, and since this happened for the sake of the Blessed Beauty, and in the pathway of the One Beloved, it behoves you to thank God and praise Him, for having singled you out for this great bounty.

For this clamour and uproar, the blows, the abuse, the taunts, the curses, when borne for love of the All-Bounteous Lord, are but festive days and times for jubilee.

God be praised, you have been given a drop out of that ocean of tribulations that swept across the Exalted One and the Beauty of the All-Glorious, you were granted a droplet out of the seas of calamity that engulfed 'Abdu'l-Bahá.

The evil ones did not destroy the Mashriqu'l-Adhkár, nor will they ever; it was their own house that they brought down in ruins and gave to the winds. They did not burn down the school, they put the flame to their own roots.

Lofty is the structure of the House of Worship; it is certain that you will build a new and greater one. Be you confident of the bestowals of the Blessed Beauty and the gifts and blessings of 'Abdu'l-Bahá.

63. THE sad news about the death of your husband has just reached us; we fully sympathize with you. When one meditates over the general trend of affairs and drinks deep from the fountain of the teachings of Bahá'u'lláh and 'Abdu'l-Bahá he is bound to come to the conclusion that this world is no world of attachment; nay rather it constantly gives us the lesson of keeping aloof as far as possible from it. This point becomes clearer now that the physical body of the Master is taken away from us. We should really congratulate the departing ones because they leave this world of pains and troubles and enter the eternal bliss of being with holy spirits which have been working to detach humanity from the ephemeral world.

64. THE letter you have written was received with the utmost joy for it was to us not only a

message of love and unity but a message of humble devotion and servitude at the divine Threshold. It was not only the cause of comfort to our broken hearts but also a divine balm to our souls and we are sure that the spirit which that letter bore is the one which reigns in the heart of each single member of that united assembly.

You have written that your number is small; but it is decidedly true that it is not numbers that count, it is, rather, the sincerity and devotion of the hearts. It is the heart that, subduing within itself all earthly cares, shines forth resplendent in the realm of love and selflessness, attracting to itself the souls of the weary and depressed, soothing their wounds with the balm of this Message. This new Revelation has in reality been the water of life unto the thirsty, a sea of knowledge unto the searcher, a message of condolence to the weary and a new spirit and life to the whole world. And now it remains that we, the humble servants of our Lord should be confirmed, through our own effort and through His bounty to diffuse this light everywhere and to carry this Glad Tidings to every cottage and princely home.

We ask God to make each one of that assembly a herald of love wherever he may go and that he may be accepted as a humble servant of His Lord.

65. ALL praise be unto the Court of Holiness, that God has drawn certain blessed souls, entities

delicate and pure, unto a realm where they have no desire save the good-pleasure of the Beloved; where, in the pathway of the Ancient Beauty and their devotion to 'Abdu'l-Bahá, they yearn for naught and have no other aim but to offer themselves up, to serve, to guide humankind, and to wander, homeless and portionless, over the earth.

Such promptings derive from the blessings and confirmations of the Abhá Kingdom. Such impulses come when a soul is cleaving fast to the eternal world. . . . As to your not being present in the Holy Land on the occasion of the anniversary of His Passing, nor able to take part with these bereaved ones in our mourning for the setting of the Sun of the Covenant: be assured that in that dread hour, that calamitous time, the souls of the people of Bahá were, one and all, circumambulating His resplendent resting-place, and the lamentation and wailing of this faithful band were continually rising up to the heavenly Throne. And that immaculate Spirit must have gazed down upon them from the realms on high, and bestowed upon them all His grace, and grieved over the grieving of them all, and consoled and soothed them all, and supplicated, even as He now supplicates, His Supreme Companion to grant unto every one of them fervour and joy, and ardour and bliss, and detachment from the world, and steadfast faith.

It is our hope that we all shall be blessed and confirmed in whatever befits this day.

66. IT has been demonstrated time and time again that whatever comes to pass only enhances the glory of God's Faith, and further proclaims His Word. This time it will be the same.

However savage this tempest of trials, however battered by surging waves the Ark of the Faith may be, still, the Divine Mariner has taken into His own two powerful hands the helm of this Ark—and He, steady, calm and able, and endowed with all authority and might, is steering its course, and will bring it at last safe and secure to its glorious haven. Of this there can be no question.

You have sent us the good news that the believers are arising to serve the Faith and are loyal and devoted to the Chosen Branch, the Guardian of the Cause of God. This news rejoiced our hearts.

We pray for you most humbly at the Holy Thresholds, and beg of God to grant His ever-increasing confirmations and blessings to all of you.

67. THE cheque for the amount of two hundred pounds that you had sent as your contribution to the Temple Fund has been received and duly forwarded to Chicago. Behold what a pervasive power this evidence of co-operation and support, this spirit of selfless consecration is bound to release in the realm of the heart and spirit. Consider to what extent the world of human virtues will be enriched and

adorned by this munificent act, and how glorious the light that this manifestation of unity and solidarity is likely to shed upon all regions. Indeed, this mighty endeavour has been accomplished despite the adverse economic situation in Persia, where the evidences of hardship, privation and depression are clearly apparent. But since the object of this noble enterprise and praiseworthy effort is to enhance the glory of the Cause of God, therefore it will unfailingly attract divine blessings and bounty.

68. It is clear and evident that the body of mankind in this day stands in dire need of such members and organs as are capable, useful and active, so that their movements and activities, their bearing and behaviour, their tender feelings, lofty sentiments and noble intentions may at all times reflect heavenly virtues and perfections and become the expressions of divine attributes and saintly characteristics, thus breathing a new life and spirit into all the dwellers of the world and causing the inner ties and spiritual relationships to be fostered and fortified in all fields of human endeavour.

69. We beseech God—exalted be His glory—to grant awareness and insight to the men of wisdom as well as to those who hold in their grasp the reins of

power in Persia, that they may be able to distinguish the right way from the crooked and devious path and may clearly discern the well-wisher from the ill-wisher with a true and genuine sense of discrimination.

As regards the amelioration of your own affairs, let us entrust the whole matter to the Blessed Beauty. He is the best Benefactor, unsurpassed in His bounty.

70. YOUR letter of 12th October 1922 is just received and refreshed in our memory the many beautiful days that you spent here when the Beloved Lord, 'Abdu'l-Bahá, was still on this earth. Those are days that many events of history could never efface from the hearts, nay rather the further we go in the scale of life the deeper become the impressions thereof within the meshes of our inner life.

I read your letter with full attention and in the course of the reading the words of the Master were ringing in my ear; words that have descended like showers on all souls and hearts that could understand. Now is the time when we should forget everything and concentrate our thoughts upon the advancement of the Cause of God and strive day and night that the principles and teachings of His Holiness Bahá'u'lláh and the words of the Master may find full expression in the hearts of the true friends.

When I think over the history of the Cause and the many difficulties that all its promoters have undergone I unhesitatingly am convinced that the sincere friends who have watched the events will not lose a moment but will with all their hearts and souls sacrifice everything of worth in order to realize that for which the Divine plan has been working.

Have all your thoughts directed to the Master and heed not what you hear from here or there. We hope that soon beloved Shoghi Effendi will come back to Haifa and things will resume their natural course. What we need today is complete unity amongst the friends and this will attract the Divine assistance from the Abhá Kingdom.

All the members of the Holy family remember you and pray for you at the Holy Shrines. We hope to hear much good news from you; this will be the Cause of the Master's happiness as He always wished to hear from you good news. Convey my Abhá greetings to all the brothers and sisters there.

71. ALL praise to the beloved Abhá Beauty, that those nightingales of the gardens of knowledge, those doves of the fragrant bowers of certitude, are singing the holy verses on the boughs of grace and bounty, celebrating the praise and glory of the Lord of the worlds, chanting His holy words, carolling to Him hymns of love, and extolling and lauding His blessed name.

God be thanked, the spirits rejoice, the hearts are full of fervour, the souls are held spellbound by that shining Face. The Blessed Beauty's sea of bounty is rolling up great waves; He is casting the rays of His grace over the world and all its peoples; the clouds of His liberal bestowals are showering down, the sun of His generosity is shining bright.

In its every aspect, this noblest of Dispensations and greatest of eras is something set apart, for it is most exalted, most glorious, and distinguished from the past. In no wise is it to be compared with the ages gone before. So plainly, in this mighty day, have the mysteries been laid bare, that to the perceptive and the initiated and those who have attained the knowledge of divine secrets, they appear as tangible realities. In this new Day the stars of allusions and hints have fallen, for the Sun of explicit texts has risen, and the Moon of expositions and interpretations has shone above all horizons.

As expressly stated in the Holy Text, a specific Centre has been given us. With His own pen has 'Abdu'l-Bahá, the Centre of the Covenant, selected and appointed Shoghi Effendi, the Chosen Branch, the Guardian of the Cause of God, the interpreter of the Book of God, so that the highway of divine guidance has been clearly marked out and lighted up for all the ages to come. This bounty is one of the distinguishing features of this mightiest of Dispensations, a special grace allotted to this age.

It is my hope that we all shall arise, thus to prove our gratitude for all these rich bestowals and gifts, and serve the Cause of God and spread the holy Teachings and speedily carry out the instructions of 'Abdu'l-Bahá—so that day by day the limits of the Faith will be extended, and the seekers will find their goal, and the lovers reach the beauty of the Beloved, and the thirsty come to crystal waters, and spiritual joys embrace mankind, and every heart be gladdened.

72. Your kind and loving letter written with an unbounded love and a sincere devotion for our beloved 'Abdu'l-Bahá and His Cause has been duly received. It spoke of that painful story where earthly cares and physical illnesses have prevented blessed souls, so overflowing with love, to shine in this dark and dismal world. Nevertheless, dear sister, rest assured and never be sorrowful. It is in one of the foremost Tablets of Bahá'u'lláh that He says: 'Verily God hath made adversity as a morning dew upon His green pasture, and a wick for His lamp which lighteth earth and heaven.' Meaning thereby that physical illnesses and misfortunes certainly make a person nearer and nearer to his Lord. Why then should we sorrow over earthly hindrances when we have done what we possibly could, and when we are sure that this, our little service, will certainly be acceptable in His Sight?

I was very glad to know that even with all these hindrances you could give the Message to certain souls and I eagerly hope that they in turn will acquire the love with which you taught them and will never stop giving this Glad Tidings to every soul they meet.

73.   PRAISE be to God that through the gracious assistance of the Abhá Kingdom those devoted friends have been enabled to achieve that which befits the glory of the Cause of God and the protection of the community of the followers of Bahá'u'lláh. This is none other than to foster unity and fellowship under all conditions, to strengthen the bonds of harmony and concord in all things, and to avoid political matters. It is particularly important to refrain from making unfavourable remarks or statements concerning the friends and the loved ones of God, inasmuch as any expression of grievance, of complaint or backbiting is incompatible with the requirements of unity and harmony and would dampen the spirit of love, fellowship and nobility. Therefore it is incumbent upon the members of the exalted Spiritual Assembly to exercise the utmost care with firm determination and not to allow the doors of complaint and grievance to be opened, or permit any of the friends to indulge in censure and backbiting. Whoever sets himself to do so, even though he be the very embodiment of the Holy Spirit, should realize that such behaviour would create disruption among the people of Bahá and would cause the standard of sedition to be raised.

In these days when the peoples of the world are thirsting for the teachings of the Abhá Beauty —teachings that provide the incomparable, life-giving waters of immortality—when we Bahá'ís have pledged ourselves to proffer these living waters to all mankind and are known to be prepared to endure every suffering and tribulation, how pitiful it would be if, despite all this, we were to neglect our binding obligations and responsibilities and to occupy ourselves with disagreeable discussions that provoke irritation and distress and to turn our attention to matters that lead to ill-feeling, to despondency and unhappiness and reduce the penetrating influence of the Word of God.

74. YOUR letter was received and its contents were perused. The scrolls you had enclosed were clearly understood. They are of no consequence whatsoever, nor are they worthy of any attention. The letter you have written in reply, although brief, is adequate and conclusive. What you have written, even as the tablet of your heart, is illumined with the light of constancy and steadfastness, and indicates your firmness and determination in upholding His Covenant. In truth this is the essential thing.

Following the ascension of 'Abdu'l-Bahá—may our lives be offered up for His holy Dust—the Covenant-breakers, using every means in their power, busied themselves in spreading false reports. No calumny, no slander did they spare. Likewise,

after the ascension of the Ancient Beauty, the Most
Great Name—may the life of all created things be
sacrificed for His holy dust—the people of doubt
and hesitation seized upon every means and arose to
destroy the edifice of the Cause, to profane the
honour of the Lord and to violate His Covenant.
Yet, during all this time and under all conditions
these bereaved and oppressed ones, with faces set
towards His luminous Threshold, held fast to the
cord of patience and resignation, engaged themselves in offering fervent prayers and supplications
and committed all their affairs to the care of the
Blessed Beauty. For in truth He is the Refuge of the
oppressed and the unfailing Comforter of the
anguished, whereas the Centre of Sedition and his
following have gathered no fruit from their rebellious acts save despondency and utter loss.

75.   IT was sometime ago that I received your
kind and encouraging letter through your honour-
able secretary. And although in a joyless world, the
love and unity of the friends in Yonkers imparted
the utmost joy to this bereaved family. Great indeed
as was my desire to reciprocate those kind sentiments so beautifully expressed in your letter, it is
truly unfortunate that I should have delayed the
answer so long.

For the last few weeks we have all been happy
over Shoghi Effendi's safe arrival and we really miss
all our beloved brethren and sisters in this little town

of Haifa. Last night's sad and solemn occasion was passed in prayer and meditation. The loved ones of that dear Master had all gathered from the countries near by to join His family in commemorating the anniversary of His passing. In a night of utter silence with the rich moonlight flooding the precincts of His Shrine, the humble devotees of 'Abdu'l-Bahá had gathered in a little group just near His Tomb; and in prayerful supplications they outpoured with their tears the woe of their hearts refilling them again with faith in His loving-kindness and high hopes for the future.

On such an occasion, dear friends, what better can we do than to realize one and all that our dear Master has for ever gone from our midst, and yet with the surest faith in His tender Spirit we should arise with one accord, aided and guided by our beloved Guardian, to dedicate our lives to the Cause for which He was a living sacrifice. Deep and painful as that thought may be, it should fill our hearts with faith in the Lord. Then and only then can we lead His Cause into a glorious victory.

76. YOU quite well realize, I presume, that Shoghi Effendi has always cherished the fondest hopes for your services to the Cause of 'Abdu'l-Bahá, and I am sure that your achievements will be great, shining brilliantly as a star. The field is world-wide and with but a noble spirit and

faith in the Lord we can carry to every home this
Message of peace and brotherhood.

77. THE Pen of the divine Ordainer has so
decreed that this house of sorrows should be encompassed by unending calamity and pain. Even before
the dark clouds of one disaster are scattered, the
lowering storm of yet a new grief takes over, casting
its darkness across the inner skies of the heart. Such
has been the lot of this broken-hearted one and the
other leaves of the Holy Tree, from earliest childhood until this hour; such has been the fruit we have
plucked from the tree of our lives.

We can see before us the Holy Shrine where lies
the blessed, riddled body of the Primal Point, and
memory of the delicate and tender remains of other
martyrs passes before our eyes. The remembrance
of the Ancient Beauty's dungeon in Ṭihrán, and
that most noble Being's exile from city to city,
culminating in the murk of the 'Akká prison, is
engraved upon our minds. The calamities, the
massive afflictions, endured by 'Abdu'l-Bahá
throughout His entire life, and His wailing at the
break of dawn are recorded for all time upon the
tablets of the soul, and those cries that rose out of His
luminous heart will linger on in the mind's ear.

It is clear, too, how the most dire of all ordeals, the
ascension of the divine Beauty, made the structure
of our existence to topple down; how being
deprived of Him consumed the very limbs of our

bodies. And when our fiery tears brought on by this were not yet dried, and the heart's wound had not healed over, then the bearer of God's decree called us to yet another anguish, that dire calamity, that terrible disaster, the passing of 'Abdu'l-Bahá. Then were we, the sorrow-stricken, thrust again into the fires of separation, and the pitch darkness of deep mourning enshrouded this family.

Beloved friends of the Blessed Beauty: what could have been the purpose of those holy Beings in enduring such agonies? Why did those precious and luminous souls accept all that hardship and pain? Any just observer will acknowledge that They had no other end in view but to better the human race, and cleanse it from the imperfections of this contingent world, and see to its advancement, and endow all peoples with the wondrous virtues of humankind. Thanks be to God's bounties, the signs of such perfections, the lights of such bestowals, have become clearly manifest throughout the world. The tree of His Cause grows ever more massive, day by day, and heavier with fruit, and from moment to moment taller, and it shall cast its wondrous shade over all who seek its shelter.

The fruit of these boughs is plain to see: this Tree will bear sincere love and true friendship, traits of Heaven and qualities of God. This immortal Tree will yield kindness and humbleness, learning and wisdom, and the divine virtues.

The aim of those blessed Ones, then, those Temples of holiness, in enduring, over a whole century, all Their trials and tribulations, was to firmly establish a way of life whereby human character in general and that of God's loved ones in particular would be rectified. To such a degree must this come to pass that from their very breathing and walking, their rising up, sitting still, moving about, their every act—it can clearly be seen that they are different from those others who are neglectful of God and veiled away from Him: that they can be distinguished from the others as easily as you can tell the day-star from the dark.

Although through the mighty influence of the Word of God the inner self of each of the friends and of those who are steadfast in His perfect Covenant is held fast by the magnet of His love, and they are known in every land by this distinguishing characteristic and are everywhere illumined by this light —still the thing to remember is this: until the accidental events which arise from the world of the trivial and the personal are completely lost in the world of the universal, that is, in the bounties and attributes of the Merciful—that true and primal glory can never be revealed as it merits, nor ever show forth the beauty with which it is endowed. Let every steadfast soul ever bear in mind the anguish of those holy Beings and the trials They endured, and because of the wrongs They suffered, and the blood of the martyrs in His path, out of pity for what has befallen God's Cause and His Law, put the good of the Cause before any other good, and its honour before any other. Let him face every problem, whether minor or major, with goodwill and purity of motive. Let him not make of God's Law, created as it was to bring about unity and love, a means of discord. 'Abdu'l-Bahá says: 'If religion be the cause of disunity, then irreligion is surely to be preferred.'

Today as well, the Chosen Branch, the Guardian of the Cause of God, is at all times waiting expectantly—and indeed, it is the most cherished desire of his heart—to see this reality, this proof of serious effort, this feature that distinguishes the Bahá'ís from all others, clearly and unmistakably revealed in the life of every single Bahá'í.

As is well known, at the time when the Day-Star of the Covenant did set, the Chosen Branch was absent from this luminous Spot, and when he received the terrifying news of that direst of ordeals, he was overcome by a grief such as no words can describe. Broken in health, his heart brimful of sorrows, he returned to this blessed place. At that time the unfaithful, with extreme perversity and at a high point of rebellion, were openly and secretly spreading their calumnies, and this behaviour of theirs added still more to the Guardian's burden of grief. He left, therefore, and spent some time in seclusion, carrying on the affairs of the Faith, seeing to its interests and its institutions, communing with God, and imploring His help.

The Lord be praised, because of the divine bounties, during his absence there were such evidences of staunchness and loyalty and high resolve and unity and love and fervour among all the friends, men and women alike, both of East and West, and in the Holy Land—that on the one hand the Centre of Sedition, and the arrogant and the malevolent, found themselves utterly defeated, their hopes of making a breach in the Faith bitterly disappointed, while on the other, the exemplary quality and sound condition of the believers, as referred to, was a comfort to the Guardian's heart. Thus he was able, happy now and in perfect health, to return to this Spot, and to carry out his sacred obligations.

By this time a great many matters of the utmost importance had accumulated, and letters were coming in continuously from individuals and communities, which for lack of time could not be dealt with individually. The Guardian therefore dispensed with replies to individuals and sent out general letters to the Spiritual Assemblies, in which in the clearest terms he set forth the obligations devolving upon all, and gave the friends his instructions. These basic spiritual guidelines were received by the believers with great delight and the utmost joy; they immediately put them into practice, and thus the preliminary steps were taken, and in every area progress was being made to an ever-increasing degree.

Now, however, as the letters continually streamed in, the contents of one or two of them showed that among some of the believers a certain ill-feeling had arisen, and further, that some did not, as they should, respect and duly defer to their

Spiritual Assembly. It is obvious what an effect this kind of news, whether implied or clearly stated, had on the Guardian's heart, and what an unfavourable reaction it produced. The result was that for the second time his health failed, and then, at the importunity of this evanescent soul and the urgent entreaties of the Holy Household and the repeated appeals of those in close association with him—he went away last summer.

This proved of the greatest benefit to him, and his health was completely restored. And then, one following the next, there came in good reports from Spiritual Assemblies everywhere, and other gatherings and groups, and also individuals, and this brought him great joy; so much so that following that summer's journey, out of his intense love for the believers, he began to correspond even with individuals; and continually, in the various meetings, he would express his satisfaction with and praise of all the servants of the Blessed Beauty's Threshold and the loyal friends of 'Abdu'l-Bahá.

Alas, however, once again in some communities, he noted from certain letters an absence of spirituality and good-fellowship among some of the friends, and a lack of respect among some for their Assemblies. Once more, as a result of this, his heart was filled with sorrow and once again he decided on departure. This lowly maidservant and the other members of the Household and all the Holy Leaves did all we could to blot away this grief from his radiant spirit. When in his presence, we would bring up all the good news that by the grace of God continued to pour in, and to speak of the staunchness, the loyalty, the love, the sacrifices of the believers both of East and West. We begged him to reconsider his decision—but to no avail.

He told us: 'My heart is sensitive. Just as I feel the ill-feeling that exists between individuals, and am injured by it, so too do I treasure the excellent qualities of the believers; indeed, I hold these dearer than words can tell. After that most dread ordeal, the one and only solace of my heart was the loyalty, the staunchness, the love of the friends for the Blessed Beauty and for 'Abdu'l-Bahá. Nothing can ever detract from the value of such excellent qualities, and I am deeply grateful to all the friends, men and women alike, for this. And yet, this love of theirs, with all its fervour, can never, by itself, bring the Ark of the Faith to the longed-for shore. It can never prove the claims of the people of Bahá to the people of the world. To safeguard the religion of God and reinforce its power, the friends must make use of effective means: their love must be so great that they worship one another, and shut any mutual ill-feeling out of their hearts.

'If, for example, the non-Bahá'ís should ask the friends, "What differentiates you from all the rest?", and if, to this, the friends answer, "In the pathway of our love for the Centre of our Faith, we would sacrifice our lives and possessions," those of the civilized world would never be content with such a reply. They would merely say: "Your love, your sacrifice for a single individual cannot possibly serve as a remedy for the chronic ills which plague society today." If the friends then answer: "Our religion provides principles and moral teachings whose value the wisest of the day cannot deny," this will be the response: "Noble principles and teachings will produce an effect on human character, and heal the mortal sicknesses which afflict society, only at such time when those who claim to believe in and support them are themselves the first to act upon them, and to demonstrate and incorporate the value and the benefits of them in their own everyday transactions and lives." Unless this comes about, there is nothing to distinguish the Bahá'ís from the rest.'

He also told us: 'The people of the world are carefully watching the Bahá'ís today, and minutely observing them. The believers must make every effort, and take the utmost care to ward off and remove any feelings of estrangement, and consider themselves duty-bound to comply with the decisions of their Spiritual Assemblies. To the same degree that ill-feeling among some of the believers has cast its shadow on my heart, to that same degree will my heart reflect their mutual agreement, understanding and loving affection, and their deference to the authority of their Spiritual Assemblies. And whenever I shall feel such lights reflected, I will at once return to the Holy Land and engage in the fulfilment of my sacred obligations.

Convey this message of mine to all the friends.'

It is now two weeks since he made this touching statement and left the Holy Land.

O dearly-loved ones of 'Abdu'l-Bahá! We know from His sacred Will that we must 'Take the greatest care of Shoghi Effendi ... that no dust of despondency and sorrow may stain his radiant nature' and that the tree of his spiritual being may bear fruit. We must ever keep this in mind, and from hour to hour we must develop our heedfulness, our love and affection, our sagacity and magnanimity.

It is the hope of this writer that the friends of God will put forth such efforts, and will so radiate their love for Him, as to light up the world; a love that will make the heart of the Guardian leap for joy, and then, God willing, he will soon come back again, so that before I close my eyes upon this life, the separation I endure will be over, and I can bid you all farewell with a happy heart.

My only joy, in these my numbered days, and the joy of the Master's consort, rests in the hands of those well-loved friends of 'Abdu'l-Bahá.

Upon you be the glory of the All-Glorious.

78.   'O God, My God! Thou hast lighted the lamp of Thy Cause with the oil of wisdom; protect it from contrary winds. The lamp is Thine and the glass is Thine, and all things in the heavens and on earth are in the grasp of Thy power.'[1]

[1] Bahá'u'lláh, *Epistle to the Son of the Wolf*, p. 104.

O servants of the Abhá Beauty's sacred Threshold, O beloved friends of 'Abdu'l-Bahá!

It is well known that from the earliest dawning of the Sun of Revelation, until the setting of the holy Covenant's Orb, the Ark of the Faith has continuously been battered by great waves of affliction, and beaten by calamity's storms. Tempest and whirlwind have ever assailed this holy Tree.

Still, the exalted Star has continued on its destined journey, and despite the piled-up clouds of hate and error, its rays of grace have illumined the whole earth.

The Ark of Salvation was made the safe refuge of the righteous, and the holy Tree was hung with bright, immortal fruit, so that the honeyed yield of the love of God is sweet on the lips of His people. Out of the grace of the Blessed Beauty, eyes began to see, and ears to hear, and through the bounty of 'Abdu'l-Bahá the spirits turned vigilant, and souls awoke, and to the hearts were divine mysteries confided, and individuals became day-springs of light.

And for ever and ever, time without end, the glance of God's bounty and bestowal is, from the hidden world above, unceasingly cast down, and He watches over us with favour and grace. It behoves us, then, to offer up thanks with every breath, and to be blissful at all times.

Although the towering citadel of God's Cause is upraised on foundations of iron, and His Word is founded on authority and power, and the loyal and firm in His Covenant, through the blessings of the Abhá Paradise, stand immovable as the mountains, and are fast-rooted in their love—still, the hurricanes of tests are mighty as well, and from every side comes the thundering roar of violent commotions and bitter trials. From these, at every moment each one of us should beg of God to defend and protect us.

Let us call to mind the clear statements and the warnings revealed by the Blessed Beauty, and the explanations and commentaries of 'Abdu'l-Bahá, particularly as found in His Will and Testament. This Testament was the last song of that Dove of the Rose-garden of Eternity, and He sang it on the branch of the Tree of bestowal and grace. It was His principal gift, indeed the greatest of all splendours that radiated forth from that Day-Star of bounty, out of the firmament of His bestowals. This Testament was the strong barricade built by the blessed hands of that wronged, that peerless One, to protect the garden of God's Faith. It was the mighty stronghold circling the edifice of the Law of God. This was an overflowing treasure which the Beloved freely gave, a goodly and precious legacy, left by Him to the people of Bahá. In all the world, no gift could equal this; no dazzling gem could rival such a precious pearl.

With His own pen, He designated as Guardian of the Cause of God, Shoghi Effendi Rabbani, the Chosen Branch, and made him the 'blest and sacred bough that hath branched out from the Twin Holy

Trees,' to be the one to whom all must turn, the centre and focus of all on earth.

In unmistakable terms did He set forth the obligations and elucidated the nature of the institutions of God's Holy Faith. He laid hold of discord's tree and brought it down. He for ever shut the door on conflicting interpretations and views. With every breath ought we to offer praise and thanks to the God of Grace for this bestowal. It is incumbent upon us to read and meditate on the contents of the Will and Testament at all times, and implore God at His Holy Threshold that He will aid us to carry out whatsoever it ordains.

A few days ago I sent out a general letter. A detailed, and recent, letter from the Guardian to all the people of Bahá was likewise sent out, and it is certain that you will be reading it; it is essential to circulate it among all the friends. What I mean is, that because of my great and spiritual love for you, the steadfast lovers of God and His Covenant, I have now set about writing this present letter as well.

I would like to remind the friends of these words from 'Abdu'l-Bahá's Will and Testament, as written down by His pen of bounty: 'No doubt every vainglorious one that purposeth dissension and discord will not openly declare his evil purposes, nay rather, even as impure gold, would he seize upon divers measures and various pretexts that he may separate the gathering of the people of Bahá.'

In another Tablet He calls on us to understand the intent of every individual by the course of his speech, and to see through his purpose. And from the Blessed Beauty: 'Place not your trust in every new arrival, and believe not every speaker.'

Over and over, in countless Tablets, do we find the like of these precepts. It is obvious that the purpose behind them is to awaken and warn the people of Bahá, so that the mighty citadel of the Cause will remain safe and secure from the plottings of those with evil intent, and the bright lamp of His Word will be shielded from the contrary winds unloosed by those who follow their evil passions and corrupt desires.

It is irrevocably decreed that whatsoever has been revealed and written down by the Supreme Pen and the holy hand of 'Abdu'l-Bahá will come to pass and be fully realized in this world, wherefore does it behove the people of Bahá, the souls attracted to His Splendour, to become all eyes and ears, and to be in body and soul and limbs and members all sagacity and prudence. Addressing the believers, Christ tells them: 'Be ye harmless as the submissive dove, and wise as the serpent.'[1]

In this momentous matter there must be no laxity, no inattention, for a whisper might become an axe laid to the root of the Tree of the Faith—a word from an ambitious soul could be a spark tossed into the harvest of the people of Bahá. We take refuge with God! May He guard us ever, from the recklessness of the insistent self.

For the harbouring of an evil purpose is a disease

[1] cf. *Matthew* 10:16.

which shuts out the individual from all the blessings of Heaven, and casts him deep into the pit of
perdition, of utter ruin. The point to make is that
anyone, high or low, rich or poor, learned or
unlettered, although to all appearances he may be
a jewel among men, and the fine flower of all that
is best—if he gives utterance to some pronouncement or speaks some word from which can be
detected the scent of self-worship, or a malicious
and evil purpose, his aim is to disintegrate the
Word of God and disperse the gathering of the
people of Bahá. From such individuals it is a
solemn obligation to turn away; it is an inescapable duty to pay no heed whatever to their claims.

The clear promises of God, both His tidings of
joy and His warnings, are being fulfilled, and it is
inevitable that just as the sweet musk-laden winds
of the Abhá Paradise are beginning to blow, and
the flames of God's love to spread, so too must
wintry blasts and icy breaths begin to fill the air.
You must therefore exert superhuman powers to
guard the Cause of God, and beg humbly and
with a contrite heart for help from the Kingdom
on High.

Although up to now, because of the dictates of
wisdom, the Will and Testament has not been in
general circulation, and has been entrusted only to
the Spiritual Assemblies of the various countries,
at this time a photocopy has been made from the
Master's original Text, which is in His own hand,
and it will soon be sent out, to increase the spirit-

ual joy of you who are essences of loyalty and trust, that every individual believer, every steadfast one in the Covenant who so desires, may read it and make a copy of it. Upon you be the Glory of the All-Glorious.

79. THE tongue of this lowly and grief-stricken maidservant is powerless to praise those loved ones of God, and the words uttered by her are wholly inadequate to pay a worthy tribute to the staunch firmness and constancy, to the spirit of love, enthusiasm and devotion that those servants of the Kingdom of God are now manifesting.

Praise be to God that through the unfailing grace of the Beauty of the All-Glorious and the manifold blessings of 'Abdu'l-Bahá each one of them is radiant as a star and shining like the moon in the plenitude of its splendour. That glorious Being, the incomparable Best-Beloved, graciously caused every one of His true servants to become as a brilliant lamp; while 'Abdu'l-Bahá, that matchless Beloved, transmuted the hearts of all those who stand unswervingly firm in His Covenant and Testament into a garden of roses—a garden embellished with the flowers of true knowledge, faith and assurance. Such evidences of divine bounty call for thanksgiving, and in appreciation for this heavenly grace and mercy it is essential to yield praise and adoration to the Peerless Lord.

Although the leaflets prepared by that faithless person,[1] teeming with falsehood, slander and calumny, proved to be a tempest of trials that swept over those regions, yet it was powerless to do any harm to trees that are deep-rooted, firm, and fixed, nor could it inflict damage on structures that are solid, mighty and strong. The blessed, the potent spirit of 'Abdu'l-Bahá will always protect and shield the holy and sanctified beings, will assist them, watch over them, and empower them to remain firm as immovable mountains.

Truly that which you have done is appropriate and the way you have reacted is highly fitting and proper, because in the Will and Testament primary emphasis has been laid on guarding and protecting the Cause of God. Thus it has been revealed: 'O ye beloved of the Lord! The greatest of all things is the protection of the true Faith of God, the preservation of His Law, the safeguarding of His Cause and service unto His Word.' Praise be to God that those blessed and enraptured souls who are enkindled with the fire of His love have been graciously assisted to preserve and shield the Faith of God.

You must have glanced at the idle words of that faithless person—words that are wholly motivated by selfish and personal interests. They are so futile, senseless and absurd that even the babes of this glorious Dispensation, rocked in their cradles, would recognize how vain and preposterous, how

---

[1] 'Abdu'l-Ḥusayn Ávárih (see *Bahá'í Administration*, Bahá'í Publishing Trust, Wilmette, pp. 137–139).

impregnated with subtle machinations they are. How much keener then must be the discernment of those distinguished beings whose substance of life has been moulded by the gracious and bountiful fingers of the Blessed Beauty and whose tree of existence has been watered and fed by the heavenly stream of His favour and providence. Surely those luminous gems whose nostrils are perfumed by the imperishable fragrance of holiness and are endued with a keen sense of perception will readily distinguish a loathsome odour, no matter how slight it may be, from the sweet-scented breeze blowing from the rose-garden of His Oneness. They will easily recognize the words of a conceited and malevolent one, though his words be wrapped up in delicate terms and phrases or take the guise of fellow-feeling, sympathy and kindly wishes, from the genuine expressions of truth and sincerity, of devotion, piety and faithfulness.

Indeed, it is true to say that malice will cause one's intelligence and understanding to fade, and the king of reason to become subservient to the satanic self and its promptings. Time and again has this matter been put to proof and the following blessed passage from the Will and Testament amply demonstrates this significant truth and serves to heighten the sense of alertness and vigilance. How wondrous is His Word: 'No doubt every vainglorious one that purposeth dissension and discord will not openly declare his evil purposes, nay rather, even as impure gold, would he seize upon divers measures and various pretexts that he may separate the gathering of the people of Bahá.'

The essential point is this: praise be to God, the way of His holy Faith is laid straight, the Edifice of the Law of God is well-founded and strong. He to whom the people of Bahá must turn, the Centre on which the concourse of the faithful must fix their gaze, the Expounder of the Holy Writings, the Guardian of the Cause of God, the Chosen Branch, Shoghi Effendi, has been clearly appointed in conformity with explicit, conclusive and unmistakable terms. The Religion of God, the laws and ordinances of God, the blessed teachings, the obligations that are binding on everyone—all stand clear and manifest even as the sun in its meridian glory. There is no hidden mystery, no secret that remains concealed. There is no room for interpretation or argument, no occasion for doubt or hesitation. The hour for teaching and service is come. It is the time for unity, harmony, solidarity and high endeavour.

At the blessed Holy Shrines we earnestly pray that divine assistance and confirmation be vouchsafed to all of us. We continually receive joyous news of the health and well-being of the Guardian of the Cause of God and eagerly hope that the night of separation may come to an end, that the period of bereavement may soon expire and his blessed person may return to this hallowed Spot with utmost joy and radiance. All the blessed leaves join this lowly maidservant in sending wondrous expressions of greeting to those loved ones of God and the handmaids of the Merciful. May the glory of the All-Glorious rest upon you!

80. THE question of Ávárih has surely come to your attention. In spite of the fact that last year, the first time that he visited this sacred Spot, he was shown the greatest kindness and love, and he was the object of every consideration and care, and everything was done to help him in every way; that when he left for Europe, as the reason for his visit was to teach the Faith, and he was favoured and praised by the Guardian, the friends in England showed him reverence to what was really an exaggerated degree, and received him with the warmest hospitality—that is, no one failed in showing him the utmost regard—still, when he returned to Cairo and busied himself with publishing his book, as it became apparent later on, he put the Assembly and the friends at odds, stirred up the mischief himself and then secretly wrote here and there that there was trouble in Cairo, and presented the situation so as to further his own ends.

The beloved Guardian at once laid hold of every possible means to quiet the dissension in Cairo, but it proved impossible because Ávárih, using all kinds of devices, prevented the reconciliation of the Assembly and the friends in that city. When the Guardian could endure this no longer and there was nothing more that he could do, with deep regret he left the Holy Land. His letter clearly shows how heavy was his heart.

Later, Ávárih left Egypt and came again to the Holy Land, and the interesting thing is that the moment he left, the misunderstandings among the friends in Cairo disappeared, and Bahá'í affairs went forward again in proper fashion, so that it became perfectly clear that he had been the cause of the disruption.

From here, too, he began to send out letters, and it would only grieve you to tell of the falsehoods and calumnies they contained. In Beirut, too, his talks and his actions were the same, and he spread the word that, God forbid, there is dissension everywhere. Accordingly, in order to protect the Cause of God, a telegram was sent to Baghdád, citing these words of the Ancient Beauty—exalted be His glory: 'Place not your trust in every new arrival, and believe not every speaker.' As a result, when he reached Baghdád, and wished to stir up mischief there, the friends, with great dignity and firmness, restrained him, and avoided his company.

The point is that although such talk and such behaviour have no effect and no importance whatsoever, and do not merit our attention, still this disloyalty of his in these days of trial and sorrow is such that, unable to bear the situation any longer, this grieved and helpless one has felt obliged to set down a brief account of what actually took place.

81. PRAISE be to God that through His gracious bounty you were enabled to visit His exalted, His sacred and luminous Threshold, to refresh and perfume your nostrils with the sweet-scented fragrances of God diffused from these imperishable, holy Places. This wondrous gift calls for thanksgiving, and this heavenly bestowal warrants praise and glorification. And such praise is best expressed when one's pilgrimage, one's honour at attaining His holy Court and becoming the recipient of His favours and loving-kindness produce a profound effect and influence upon every aspect of one's life, upon one's bearing and demeanour, and one's activities. There is no doubt that it will be so.

82. IT is a very long time since we have had any news from you and we are quite longing to have one of your interesting and beautiful letters, that brings us always comfort because of your sincerity, your love for the Cause and your constant energy in the work for the Cause. You have ever been one of the Master's best friends, you are one of the oldest American believers, one of the firm and enthusiastic workers, and we are always happy to hear from you. The joy of our hearts is to hear that the friends are active and sincere in the spreading of the teachings.

We always long to hear about the friends, to know that in America they are arising with sincere energy to assist our beloved Guardian, to make his heart happy so that he may return to the Holy Land and again take up, with renewed vigour, the burdens that are too great when he feels that the friends are not uniting with him to carry out the instructions of the Beloved. We know that these instructions and teachings are the balm for the wounds and ills of the world, and if the friends are not firm, sincere and united in the principles as given by Bahá'u'lláh, explained and amplified by 'Abdu'l-Bahá, and do not teach them clearly and keep them pure and unadulterated, then how can the ills of mankind be alleviated? All other teachings have failed to eliminate the existing prejudices between peoples and religions and unite them upon the basis of pure truth, and now that we have this blessed remedy which is a divine solvent, let us not be blind or neglectful, but energetically and courageously stand forth as true heralds of this Divine Remedy.

83. YOUR short and loving note of June 25th has been received. Its contents, though short, gave me and the ladies of the Household great joy, because they indicate that the dear friends have, with willing efforts, arisen to strengthen the foundation of love and harmony in their hearts. This will surely release our beloved Shoghi Effendi from his grief, fill his dear heart with joy and bring him to us again.

Since my last affectionate appeal to the beloved of God and 'Abdu'l-Bahá's spiritual children, the dear friends in every land have indeed shown a wonderful spirit which has inspired us all with joy and gratitude. For their confirmation and success we ardently pray at the Holy Shrines. I hope and pray that your National Spiritual Assembly will this year be favoured with divine support and unprecedented prosperity.

84. YOUR charming letter of June 20th has arrived and with it the spiritual waves of your love and devotion to the welfare of the Cause of God and to the prosperity of the dear friends throughout America.

I pray at the Holy Shrine of our beloved Lord, 'Abdu'l-Bahá, to favour you with the realization of the desire of your heart which contributes to the joy and happiness of the beloved Guardian of the Cause, that is, service towards the unity of the dear friends and the promulgation of the divine Teachings which alone can redeem this lifeless world.

I am glad to tell you that the Guardian of the Cause of God is in good health. The splendid attitude of the beloved friends in the East and the West and their wonderfully sacrificial efforts in the service of the Cause have greatly lightened the burden of grief upon his loving heart and so, he may return to the Holy Land towards the end of summer when his entire grief, we hope, will be replaced with joy and fragrances which are being wafted to his dear heart.

85. YOUR numerous letters written to the beloved Guardian and myself have all arrived and brought with them the sweet perfume of your devotion, sincerity, strong faith and active and beautiful services you are inexhaustibly rendering to the Cause of God. You should be happy, dear Bahá'í sister in being so wonderfully confirmed in your spiritual life.

The beloved Guardian of the Cause is nowadays in good health and through the magnificent efforts the friends are exerting in every country to strengthen and augment their bond of unity and love for one another, his grief has been lightened and so we have great hope that he will return to the Holy Land before long. Here he will resume his personal touch with the friends the world over and will inspire them with his guidance to still greater activity.

The Ladies of the Holy Family and I are always remembering you dear friends of 'Abdu'l-Bahá and praying for your confirmation and happiness. I am thankful to all the dear friends who so faithfully and lovingly responded with their excellent deeds to my affectionate appeal for greater unity and love. May the Blessed Beauty and 'Abdu'l-Bahá reward them richly and crown their sincere services with great results.

86. FROM this hallowed Spot I send heavenly greetings to those two faithful servants of the holy Threshold of the Abhá Beauty. Indeed, no word of

compliment could be compared to this expression of praise and commendation, whereby, thanks be to God, you both have distinguished yourselves as the devoted servants of His divine Threshold and as the sincere, the self-sacrificing bond-slaves serving at the door of His mercifulness. You have always proved yourselves untiring in your noble efforts and are continually striving with utmost endeavour to discharge your important and glorious duties. This can be attributed to naught save to the unfailing bounties of the Abhá Beauty and to the invisible aid that 'Abdu'l-Bahá has graciously accorded you.

87.   IN this Day nothing is so important as service. Did not 'Abdu'l-Bahá voluntarily call Himself the 'Servant' of Bahá, manifesting also in His life the perfections of servitude to God and man?

We, wishing to follow the commands left by Bahá'u'lláh, spread and lived by 'Abdu'l-Bahá, we can take no greater step toward the Heavenly Kingdom—can give no greater joy to the present beloved Guardian of the Cause, Shoghi Effendi—than that of loving service to all mankind.

88.   IT always cheers my heart to hear from the dear friends whose hearts are so full of love and devotion, and desire to serve this Blessed Cause which has been proclaimed by Bahá'u'lláh to all the world, so that all national, racial, and religious

prejudices will be abolished, and the world of humanity recognized as one home, and all men as brothers.

I certainly shall pray specially for you that you may be richly blessed in your work and service to the Blessed Cause. One soul who becomes entirely selfless and devoted and filled to overflowing with the spirit of love and service will do much for the progress of the Cause in whatever locality he is. Be assured, if you arise to serve, the Beloved Master says *Nothing shall be impossible to you if you have faith. As ye have faith so shall your powers and blessings be.* I convey to you the warm love and Bahá'í greetings of Shoghi Effendi, and all the family, and again assure you of our earnest prayers that you will be enabled to render much service to the Kingdom.

89. My heart is always cheered when I meet or hear from the dear friends in America, for the Beloved Master spoke so much to us about His visit to your land, and we feel confident that the teachings of the Blessed Perfection which He heralded forth have not fallen on barren soil and the day is not far distant when a rich harvest will be garnered therefrom.

90. At the holy Threshold of the Abhá Beauty we fervently pray at all times for outstanding success to attend that exalted body.[1] Indeed, by virtue of the

[1] The Local Spiritual Assembly of Ṭihrán.

brilliant achievements won and the distinguished services rendered by those blessed souls, the heart of this lowly one is filled with utmost joy and assurance, and there is no doubt that through the loving-kindness of God this measure of joy and happiness will be multiplied day by day.

You have asked me about my own knowledge and recollections concerning the holy Houses in Ṭihrán. Unfortunately, due to my tender age at that time, those blessed places and quarters have faded from my memory.

Upon you be His glory and praise.

91. O DEAR sisters, ardent lovers of Bahá'u'-lláh, may my soul be offered up for your devotion, your staunchness, and your steadfastness!

The letter from the honoured members of that spiritual assemblage, telling of the women of that land, their fervour, their fiery love for God, their services to His Cause, their unity and mutual kindness and loving fellowship, their grieving over the departure of the world's Day-Star—has reached this afflicted one. Reading it, I begged most humbly of our Living and Eternal Lord, to aid and bless those handmaids at all times and under all conditions. He is verily the One Who is near to us all, and answers our prayers.

To us who sorrow here, there is truly no joy in life save only the good news that the lovers of God and of 'Abdu'l-Bahá, may my life be sacrificed for the

Spot which enshrines His holy Dust, are steadfast and firm, and that those loyal handmaids have girded themselves to serve the Faith, and casting aside on the pathway of God their ease and comfort, are proclaiming the Teachings, calling souls to life, and making sure that the sacred blood of the Primal Point, the afflictions and the captivity of the Abhá Beauty, the anguish of 'Abdu'l-Bahá shall through you, men and women alike, through your steadfastness today, yield goodly fruit for all on earth to see.

I presented your letter to the Chosen Branch, the Guardian of the Faith, Shoghi Effendi, and upon reading it he expressed great joy and satisfaction. He expressed gratitude to the Lord that men and women have been raised up and are gathered beneath the banner of the Covenant, every one of whom, in the field of divine knowledge, can put armies of error to flight. Through souls such as these is God's promise fulfilled: '*We shall aid whosoever will arise for the triumph of our Cause with the hosts of the Concourse on high and a company of Our favoured angels.*'

92. Your letter, laden with many a graceful phrase, many a wondrous inner meaning, has been received. Its perusal brought composure and tranquillity to my soul and gladness to my heart, inasmuch as from between its lines I could discern the tokens of your unswerving constancy in God's Mighty Cause and of your intense devotion to the

almighty Lord. I beseech God to illumine your heart with the light of His love, to unloose your tongue in magnifying His praise and in extolling His glory, to strengthen you with so mighty a power that you may vindicate the truth of His Faith by expounding infallible proofs and conclusive testimonies.

You have told me about your taking part in special gatherings for the training of Persian and American Bahá'í children. Excellent indeed is what you have done. Rest well assured, O handmaid of God, in the gracious favour of your Lord. Verily He will sustain you in your efforts for the advancement of His Cause and in rendering service to the world of humanity. Exert your utmost endeavour, and expend whatever is dear to you in this glorious path that you may earn the crown of righteousness, imperishable and everlasting.

Indeed the peoples of the world spend their days in idle imaginings, wholly oblivious to the Truth. Know of a certainty that the ornament of life is to be arrayed with the vesture of praiseworthy conduct and be attired with the crown of goodly deeds.

All the members of the family and myself are enjoying excellent health and we send our loving greetings and best wishes to you and to all the beloved friends there. I earnestly beseech from His holy Threshold that He may purge you from every affliction, grant you perfect health and may aid you to serve His sublime Cause in this glorious Day.

VI

DOCUMENTATION

VI

DOCUMENTATION

LIST OF SOURCES

I. *From the Writings of Bahá'u'lláh*

Dedicatory Passage. From a Tablet addressed to the Greatest Holy Leaf, inscribed in the original Arabic on her Monument. (See *The Bahá'í World*, vol. V, p. 171)

1. From a Tablet addressed to the Greatest Holy Leaf. (See *The Bahá'í World*, vol. V, p. 171)
2. From an unpublished Tablet addressed to the Greatest Holy Leaf

II. *From the Writings of 'Abdu'l-Bahá*

1. From a Tablet addressed to the Greatest Holy Leaf. (See *The Bahá'í World*, vol. V, pp. 171–172)
2. From a Tablet addressed to the Greatest Holy Leaf. (See *The Bahá'í World*, vol. V, p. 172)
3. From a Tablet addressed to the Greatest Holy Leaf. (See *The Bahá'í World*, vol. V, p. 172)

4. From a Tablet addressed to the Greatest Holy Leaf. (See *The Bahá'í World*, vol. V, p. 172)

5. From a Tablet addressed to the Greatest Holy Leaf. (See *The Bahá'í World*, vol. V, p. 172)

6. From a Tablet addressed to Munírih Khánum, the wife of 'Abdu'l-Bahá. (See *The Bahá'í World*, vol. V, p. 172)

7. From a Tablet addressed to Díyá'íyyih Khánum, eldest daughter of 'Abdu'l-Bahá. (See *The Bahá'í World*, vol. V, p. 172)

8. From an unpublished Tablet addressed to the Greatest Holy Leaf

9. From an unpublished Tablet addressed to the Greatest Holy Leaf

10. From an unpublished Tablet addressed to the Greatest Holy Leaf

11. From an unpublished Tablet addressed to the Greatest Holy Leaf

12. From an unpublished Tablet addressed to the Greatest Holy Leaf

13. From an unpublished Tablet addressed to Hájí Mírzá Hasan-i-Khurásání

14. From an unpublished Tablet addressed to the Greatest Holy Leaf

15. From an unpublished Tablet addressed to the Greatest Holy Leaf

16. From an unpublished Tablet addressed to the Greatest Holy Leaf

17. From an unpublished Tablet addressed to the Greatest Holy Leaf

18. From an unpublished Tablet addressed to the Greatest Holy Leaf

19. From an unpublished Tablet addressed to the Greatest Holy Leaf

20. From an unpublished Tablet addressed to the Greatest Holy Leaf

21. From an unpublished Tablet addressed to Munírih Khánum

III. *From the Writings of Shoghi Effendi*

Unless otherwise specified the following excerpts are from letters addressed to individual believers.

1. April 1922, announcement to the Bahá'ís in the west. (Translated from the Persian) (See *Star of the West*, vol. 13, pp. 81–82, and *Bahá'í Administration*, p. 25)

2. 21 March 1932, to the Bahá'ís of the United States and Canada. (See *The World Order of Bahá'u'lláh*, pp. 67–68)

3. 15 July 1932, to the National Spiritual Assembly of the Bahá'ís of the United States and Canada. (See *Messages to America*, p. 1)

4. 15 July 1932, to the National Spiritual Assembly of the Bahá'ís of the British Isles

5. 3 Kalimát 89 (15 July 1932 A.D.), to the Bahá'ís of the East. (Translated from the Persian)

6. 17 July 1932, to the Bahá'ís of the West. (See *Bahá'í Administration*, 1974 edn., pp. 187–196)

7. 18 July 1932, to the National Spiritual Assembly of the Bahá'ís of the United States and Canada

8. 18 July 1932

9. 1 August 1932, to the National Spiritual Assembly of the Bahá'ís of the United States and Canada

10. 15 August 1932

11. 23 August 1932

12. 23 August 1932, to the Spiritual Assembly of the Bahá'ís of Yonkers, N.Y.

13. 25 August 1932

14. 30 August 1932, to the Spiritual Assembly of the Bahá'ís of Berkeley, California

15. 30 August 1932, to the Spiritual Assembly of the Bahá'ís of Racine, Wisconsin

16. 1 September 1932, to the Bahá'ís of Washington, D.C.

17. 1 September 1932, to the National Spiritual Assembly of the Bahá'ís of the United States and Canada

18. 5 September 1932. (Translated from the Persian)

19. 10 September 1932, to the Bahá'ís of Glendale, California

20. 10 September 1932, to the National Spiritual Assembly of the Bahá'ís of the United States and Canada

21. 10 September 1932

22. 11 October 1932, to the Spiritual Assembly of the Bahá'ís of Teaneck, New Jersey

23. 27 October 1932, to the National Spiritual Assembly of the Bahá'ís of the United States and Canada

24. 2 Masá'il 89 (13 December 1932 A.D.), to the Bahá'ís of Iran. (Translated from the Persian)

25. 14 January 1933, to the Bahá'ís of the United States and Canada

26. 21 April 1933, to the Bahá'ís of the United States and Canada. (See *The World Order of Bahá'u'lláh*, pp. 81–82)

27. 8 February 1934, to the Bahá'ís of the West. (See *The World Order of Bahá'u'lláh*, p. 98)

28. 25 December 1938, to the Bahá'ís of the United

States and Canada. (See *The Advent of Divine Justice*, p. 37)

29. 5 December 1939, to the Bahá'ís of the United States and Canada
30. 25 December 1939, to the Bahá'ís of the East. (Translated from the Persian)
31. 1944, *God Passes By*, p. 108
32. 1944, *God Passes By*, p. 347
33. 27 November 1954, to the Bahá'ís of the World. (See *Messages to the Bahá'í World*, p. 74)

IV. *From Letters written in English on behalf of Shoghi Effendi by his Persian secretaries*

Unless otherwise specified the following excerpts are from letters addressed to individual believers.

1. 15 August 1932
2. 23 August 1932
3. 23 August 1932, to the Spiritual Assembly of the Bahá'ís of Yonkers, N.Y.
4. 25 August 1932
5. 30 August 1932, to the Spiritual Assembly of the Bahá'ís of Berkeley, California
6. 30 August 1932, to the Spiritual Assembly of the Bahá'ís of Racine, Wisconsin
7. 30 August 1932
8. 1 September 1932, to the Bahá'ís of Washington, D.C.
9. 5 September 1932. (Translated from the Persian)

10. 9 September 1932. (Translated from the Persian)
11. 9 September 1932. (Translated from the Persian)
12. 10 September 1932, to the Bahá'ís of Jacksonville, Florida
13. 10 September 1932, to the Bahá'ís of Monroe, Washington
14. 10 September 1932, to the National Spiritual Assembly of the Bahá'ís of the United States and Canada
15. 15 September 1932. (Translated from the Persian)
16. 15 September 1932. (Translated from the Persian)
17. 15 September 1932, to the Spiritual Assembly of the Bahá'ís of Shíráz. (Translated from the Persian)
18. 15 September 1932, to the National Spiritual Assembly of the Bahá'ís of the United States and Canada
19. 4 October 1932, to the Bahá'ís of Australia
20. 4 October 1932, to the Spiritual Assembly of the Bahá'ís of Phoenix, Arizona
21. 6 October 1932
22. 7 October 1932
23. 8 October 1932, to the Spiritual Assembly of the Bahá'ís of Adelaide, Australia
24. 10 October 1932
25. 11 October 1932, to the Bahá'ís of Teaneck, New Jersey
26. 18 October 1932
27. 29 October 1932
28. 9 November 1932
29. 9 November 1932
30. 30 November 1932
31. 15 March 1933
32. 29 May 1933, to the Bahá'ís of Bournemouth, England
33. 6 March 1945. (Translated from the Persian)

V. *From Letters of the Greatest Holy Leaf*

Unless otherwise specified the following excerpts are from letters addressed to individual believers.

1. See facsimile of original, facing page 157
2. 12 Muḥarram 1307 A.H. (8 September 1889 A.D.)
3. 14 S̲h̲avvál 1310 A.H. (1 May 1893 A.D.)
4. Dhi'l-Qa'dih 1314 A.H. (3 April–2 May 1897 A.D.)
5. 9 Muḥarram 1315 A.H. (10 June 1897 A.D.)
6. Dhi'l-Ḥijjih 1316 A.H. (12 April–11 May 1899 A.D.)
7. Dhi'l-Ḥijjih 1316 A.H. (12 April–11 May 1899 A.D.)
8. 7 Muḥarram 1317 A.H. (18 May 1899 A.D.)
9. Dhi'l-Qa'dih 1318 A.H. (20 February–21 March 1901 A.D.)
10. Undated, postmarked 9 April 1901
11. Dhi'l-Qa'dih 1321 A.H. (19 January–17 February 1904 A.D.), to a believer in Ṭihrán
12. Jamádíyu'th-T̲h̲ání 1322 A.H. (13 August–10 September 1904 A.D.), to a Bahá'í family
13. Ṣafar 1323 A.H. (7 April–5 May 1905 A.D.)
14. Dhi'l-Qa'dih 1323 A.H. (28 December 1905–26 January 1906 A.D.), to a believer in Yazd
15. Ṣafar 1325 A.H. (16 March–13 April 1907 A.D.)
16. 1 January 1921
17. Undated, to the President of the Bahá'í Women's Society in Chicago
18. Undated
19. Undated
20. Undated
21. 28 November 1921, to the Executive Board of Bahá'í Temple Unity
22. 14 December 1921 (date received), to the Executive Board of Bahá'í Temple Unity

23. 22 December 1921 (date received), to the Executive Board of Bahá'í Temple Unity
24. 17 January 1922 (date received), to the Executive Board of Bahá'í Temple Unity
25. Sha'bán 1340 A.H. (30 March–28 April 1922 A.D.), to the Servants of the Blessed Beauty and the dear friends of 'Abdu'l-Bahá. (See *Star of the West*, vol. 13, pp. 82–83)
26. Feast of Riḍván 1922 (21 April–2 May 1922 A.D.), to the friends in America. (See *Star of the West*, vol. 13, p. 88)
27. 1 May 1922 (date received), to the National Spiritual Assembly of the Bahá'ís of the United States and Canada
28. Ramaḍán 1340 A.H. (28 April–27 May 1922 A.D.), to a believer in Ṭihrán
29. Ramadán 1340 A.H. (28 April–27 May 1922 A.D.), to the Bahá'ís in Iran
30. Ramaḍán 1340 A.H. (28 April–27 May 1922 A.D.), to a believer in Tabríz
31. Ramaḍán 1340 A.H. (28 April–27 May 1922 A.D.), to a Bahá'í family in Tabríz
32. Ramaḍán 1340 A.H. (28 April–27 May 1922 A.D.), to a believer in Qazvín
33. Ramaḍán 1340 A.H. (28 April–27 May 1922 A.D.), to the Spiritual Assembly of the Bahá'ís of Tabríz
34. Shavvál 1340 A.H. (28 May–25 June 1922 A.D.), to the Bahá'ís in Khúsif
35. Shavvál 1340 A.H. (28 May–25 June 1922 A.D.)
36. Shavvál 1340 A.H. (28 May–25 June 1922 A.D.), to a believer in Tabríz
37. Shavvál 1340 A.H. (28 May–25 June 1922 A.D.), to the Spiritual Assembly of the Bahá'ís of Ardikán
38. Shavvál 1340 A.H. (28 May–25 June 1922 A.D.), to a believer in Karachi

39. 26 Shavvál 1340 A.H. (22 June 1922 A.D.), to a believer in Qazvín

40. Dhi'l-Qa'dih 1340 A.H. (26 June–25 July 1922 A.D.), to a believer in Míyánaj

41. Dhi'l-Qa'dih 1340 A.H. (26 June–25 July 1922 A.D.), to a believer in Shíráz

42. Dhi'l-Qa'dih 1340 A.H. (26 June–25 July 1922 A.D.), to the Bahá'ís in Khurásán

43. Dhi'l-Qa'dih 1340 A.H. (26 June–25 July 1922 A.D.), to the Friends of God

44. Dhi'l-Qa'dih 1340 A.H. (26 June–25 July 1922 A.D.), to a believer in Khurásán

45. 12 Dhi'l-Qa'dih 1340 A.H. (7 July 1922 A.D.), to a believer in Tákur, Núr

46. 15 Dhi'l-Qa'dih 1340 A.H. (10 July 1922 A.D.), to the Bahá'ís of Husayn-Ábád, Yazd

47. 19 Dhi'l-Qa'dih 1340 A.H. (14 July 1922 A.D.), to the Bahá'ís of Míyánaj

48. 22 Dhi'l-Qa'dih 1340 A.H. (17 July 1922 A.D.), to a believer in 'Ishqábád, Turkistán

49. 20 July 1922, to the Bahá'ís in America

50. 4 August 1922, to the Bahá'ís in the West

51. 15 Dhi'l-Hijjih 1340 A.H. (8 August 1922 A.D.), to a believer in Tihrán

52. 9 August 1922

53. 10 August 1922, to a believer in Alexandria, Egypt

54. 20 Muharram 1341 A.H. (12 September 1922 A.D.)

55. 22 Muharram 1341 A.H. (14 September 1922 A.D.), to a believer in Khurásán

56. 22 Muharram 1341 A.H. (14 September 1922 A.D.), to the members of the Spiritual Assembly of Shíshaván, a village in Ádhirbáyján

57. 24 Muharram 1341 A.H. (16 September 1922 A.D.), to the Bahá'ís of Gáv-Gán, a village near Tabríz

58. 1 Ṣafar 1341 A.H. (23 September 1922 A.D.), to a believer in Ṭihrán

59. 22 Ṣafar 1341 A.H. (14 October 1922 A.D.), to a believer in Ṭihrán

60. 2 Rabí'u'l-Avval 1341 A.H. (23 October 1922 A.D.)

61. 2 Rabí'u'l-Avval 1341 A.H. (23 October 1922 A.D.), to the Spiritual Assembly of the Bahá'ís of Ṭihrán

62. 5 Rabí'u'l-Avval 1341 A.H. (26 October 1922 A.D.), to a believer in Iṣfahán

63. 5 Rabí'u'l-Avval 1341 A.H. (26 October 1922 A.D.), to the Maidservants of the Blessed Beauty in Sang-i-Sar

64. 25 November 1922

65. Undated, to the friends in Yonkers, New York. (See *Star of the West*, vol. 13, p. 220, of November 1922)

66. 2 December 1922, to a believer in Egypt

67. 15 Rabí'u'th-Thání 1341 A.H. (5 December 1922 A.D.), to a believer in Ṭihrán

68. 15 Rabí'u'th-Thání 1341 A.H. (5 December 1922 A.D.), to the members of the Spiritual Assembly of the Bahá'ís of Ṭihrán

69. 15 Rabí'u'th-Thání 1341 A.H. (5 December 1922 A.D.), to the members of the Chicago Temple Fund Committee in Ṭihrán

70. 25 Rabí'u'th-Thání 1341 A.H. (15 December 1922 A.D.)

71. 11 December 1922

72. 23 July 1923

73. 9 Ṣafar 1342 A.H. (21 September 1923 A.D.), to the members of the Spiritual Assembly of the Bahá'ís of Shíráz

74. 4 Rabí'u'th-Thání 1342 A.H. (14 November 1923 A.D.), to a believer in Tihrán
75. 28 November 1923, to the Spiritual Assembly of the Bahá'ís of Yonkers, New York
76. 3 December 1923
77. 21 Sha'bán 1342 A.H. (28 March 1924 A.D.), to the members of the Spiritual Assemblies and all the Friends of God in the East
78. 3 Shavvál 1342 A.H. (8 May 1924 A.D.), to the Friends of God and the Maidservants of the Merciful
79. 27 May 1924, to the Spiritual Assembly of the Bahá'ís of Hamadán
80. 24 Shavvál 1342 A.H. (29 May 1924 A.D.), to a believer in Tihrán
81. 14 August 1924
82. 28 June 1924
83. 19 July 1924
84. 19 July 1924
85. 18 August 1924
86. 15 June 1925, to a Bahá'í couple in Stuttgart, Germany
87. 8 October 1924
88. 13 May 1928
89. 12 March 1929
90. 4 Jamádíyu'l-Avval 1348 A.H. (8 October 1929 A.D.), to the Spiritual Assembly of the Bahá'ís of Tihrán
91. Undated, to the Maidservants of the Merciful in Ábádih
92. Undated

VII

NOTES ON TRANSLATIONS

VII

NOTES ON TRANSLATIONS

Passages Translated by Shoghi Effendi

Passage from the Writings of Bahá'u'lláh used as a
    dedication (p. v)
Section I: No. 1
Section II: Nos. 1, 2, 3, 4, 5, 6, 7 & 12 (address and last
    paragraph, see *The Bahá'í World*, vol. V, p. 172)

Passage Translated by Zia Baghdadi

Section III: No. 1

Passages Translated by Marzieh Gail

Section II: Nos. 8, 9, 10, 11, 12 (1st and 2nd paragraphs
    only), 13, 14, 15, 16, 17, 18 & 19
Section III: Nos. 5, 18, 24 & 30

Section IV: Nos. 9, 10, 11, 15, 16 & 33
Section V: Nos. 11, 17, 25, 28, 29, 30, 31, 33, 34, 35,
    36, 37, 38, 39, 40, 41, 42, 44, 45, 46, 49, 52, 54, 55,
    56, 57, 61, 62, 65, 66, 71, 77, 78, 80 & 91

Passages Translated by a Committee at the World Centre

Section I: No. 2
Section II: Nos. 20 & 21
Section IV: No. 17
Section V: Nos. 2, 3, 4, 5, 6, 7, 8, 9, 12, 13, 14, 15, 18,
    19, 20, 32, 43, 47, 50, 53, 58, 59, 60, 67, 68, 69, 73,
    74, 79, 81, 86, 90 & 92

VIII

SOME REFERENCES TO THE GREATEST HOLY LEAF FOUND IN PUBLISHED WORKS

VIII

SOME REFERENCES TO THE GREATEST HOLY LEAF FOUND IN PUBLISHED WORKS

Bahá'u'lláh and 'Abdu'l-Bahá *Tablets Revealed in Honor of the Greatest Holy Leaf* (New York: National Spiritual Assembly of the Bahá'ís of the United States and Canada, 1933).

Shoghi Effendi:

Advent of Divine Justice, The (Wilmette: Bahá'í Publishing Trust, 1974), p. 37.

Bahá'í Administration (Wilmette: Bahá'í Publishing Trust, 1980), pp. 25, 57, 70, 93, 187–196.

The Dawn-Breakers (Wilmette: Bahá'í Publishing Trust, 1974), dedication.

God Passes By (Wilmette: Bahá'í Publishing Trust, 1974), pp. 108, 347, 350, 392.

Guidance for Today and Tomorrow (London: Bahá'í Publishing Trust, 1973), pp. 58–71.

Messages to America: Selected Letters and Cablegrams

Addressed to the Bahá'ís of North America 1932–1946 (Wilmette: Bahá'í Publishing Trust Committee, 1947), pp. 1, 31, 37.

Messages to the Bahá'í World (Wilmette: Bahap"í Publishing Trust, 1971), p. 74.

World Order of Bahá'u'lláh, The (Wilmette: Bahá'í Publishing Trust, 1980), pp. 67–68, 81–82, 93–94, 98.

Others:

Balyuzi, H. M. *'Abdu'l-Bahá, the Centre of the Covenant of Bahá'u'lláh* (Oxford: George Ronald, 1973), pp. 12, 54–55, 74, 332, 401, 416, 454–455, 463–464, 482.

Balyuzi, H. M. *Edward Granville Browne and the Bahá'í Faith* (Oxford: George Ronald, 1980), pp. 119–120.

Blomfield, Sarah, Lady, *The Chosen Highway* (Wilmette: Bahá'í Publishing Trust, 1967), pp. 37–69, 73.

Gail, Marzieh *Khanúm, the Greatest Holy Leaf, as Remembered by Marzieh Gail* (Oxford: George Ronald, 1982.

Maxwell, May *An Early Pilgrimage* (Oxford: George Ronald 1974), pp. 18–19.

Muhájir, Írán Furútan, comp. *The Mystery of God* (London: Bahá'í Publishing Trust, 1979), pp. 278–304.

Nakhjavání, Bahíyyih *Response* (Oxford: George Ronald, 1981), pp. 30–35, 40–41.

Rabbani, Rúhíyyih *The Priceless Pearl* (London: Bahá'í Publishing Trust, 1969), pp. 6–7, 10–11, 13–15, 21–22, 39, 44, 46–51, 57–58, 63, 90, 102–103, 112, 115, 129–130, 139–140, 144–148, 151–152, 168, 199, 218, 236, 259, 261–262, 266–267, 273, 279–280, 430, 438.

Universal House of Justice *Bahá'í Holy Places at the World Centre* (Haifa: Bahá'í World Centre, 1968), pp. 62–70.

The Bahá'í World, an International Record
vol. II, 1926–1928, pp. 83, 132.
vol. III, 1928–1930, p. 64.
vol. V, 1932–1934, pp. 22–23, 114–115, 169–188.
vol. VIII, 1938–1940, pp. 5, 8, 206, 255–256, 262, 266.
vol. IX, 1940–1944, p. 329.
vol. X, 1944–1946, p. 536.
vol. XI, 1946–1950, pp. 474, 492.
vol. XVI, 1973–1976, pp. 54, 66, 73.

Bahá'í News, published by the National Spiritual Assembly of the Bahá'ís of the United States and Canada
no. 18, June 1927, p. 5.
no. 36, December 1929, p. 1.
no. 52, May 1931, pp. 1–2.
no. 62, May 1932, p. 2.
no. 65, August 1932, pp. 1–2.
no. 66, September 1932, p. 1.
no. 72, March 1933, p. 3.
no. 121, December 1938, p. 3.
no. 124, April 1939, p. 1.
no. 128, August 1939, p. 4.
no. 133, February 1940, p. 1.
no. 135, April 1940, insert.

Star of the West (Chicago: Bahá'í News Service)
vol. 10, no. 17, pp. 312–314.

(Many of these references are accounts of early pilgrimages, and give only a brief mention of the Greatest Holy Leaf.)